SOCCER TRAINING:
DEVELOPING THE 360° PLAYER
by Martin Bidzinski

Library of Congress
Cataloging - in - Publication Data

Soccer Training: Developing the 360° Player
by Martin Bidzinski

ISBN-13: 978-1-59164-116-2
ISBN-10: 1-59164-116-0
Library of Congress Control Number: 2010935659
© 2010

Editing, Layout, Cover Design and Diagrams
Bryan R. Beaver

Printed by
Data Reproductions
Auburn, Michigan

Reedswain Publishing
88 Wells Road
Spring City, PA 19475
www. reedswain.com
info@reedswain.com

TABLE OF CONTENTS

PROLOGUE:
FIFA WORLD CUP™ 2010 OBSERVATIONS -
SKILL REIGNS SUPREME

For me or anyone who promotes the skills side of the game, the events of FIFA World Cup™ 2010 in South Africa were a godsend. Teams relying heavily on physicality, what I call the battling attributes, suffered at the skilled feet and creative offensive movement of teams such as Argentina, Ghana, Uruguay, Germany and eventual finalists Spain and Holland. If you wanted to see what style of play was more effective then look no further than the final match. Holland had earned their reputation over the years on the more skilful game of soccer and up to the final had stayed true to that reputation. So nothing could have surprised me more than the way they played the Spanish team in what should have been a great final. Although the Dutch could have won the game as far as I was concerned, they had sold out on their good reputation and resorted to battling attributes and intimidation against a Spain side that plainly believed in playing soccer in a skilful manner. Spain won the World Cup by staying faithful to their style of play. Also there is the case of Brazil. Brazil has won more World Cups than any other nation and is revered worldwide for it's beautiful, fluid, skilful attacking style of play. But in South Africa, Brazil adopted a more conservative, dare I say English, style under the direction of Dunga. A physical, defend first, counter attacking style certainly did not serve Brazil in the end, as they lost to the then skilful, attack minded Dutch.

Watching players in South Africa has shown me the difference between good teams and teams that struggle to win. One of the biggest problems for any player lacking a first touch repertoire is that very often he simply reverts to doing as he was 'Coached' over his many years of training. It should be understood that there are common factors between all players in terms of their development/training the world over. All players have, for example, played 'Tennis Soccer', all players have at some point been introduced to a conditioned game of soccer such as two touch or one touch drills. It is also true to say that most players are one footed and have a problem with their so-called weak side, in effect limiting their options on the ball by half. The differences between the great sides and the not so great sides as I see it are these:

1 – The great sides have players that are more mobile physically and as a result are ball friendly. In other words they can move better physically and they can handle the ball better on their first touch.

2 – The fact that they are physically more mobile and have a better playing repertoire gives them the opportunity to play a more fluent game of soccer.

The fluency in their play gives them the better platform for the offensive side of the game. They are 360° players.

That being said, however, on even the great sides the majority of players are out and out one footed. One player who provided several examples of the playing limitations of being almost exclusively one-footed is Holland star striker Arjen Robben. Blessed with great pace, vision and a cracking left foot, Robben has established himself as a world star. But how much better would he be were he more comfortable on his right foot? Numerous times in this World Cup I watched world class players like Robben squander opportunities because they either did not recognize or simply could not perform certain playing options that required the use of their "weaker" foot. I have recognized these shortcomings for years now, at all levels of the game, and have committed my coaching life to bringing about real change in the way young players are developed and selected. Too many players are left out because they lack the necessary physicality to employ the battling game. These players often leave the game at a young age, most never to return. This is a travesty.

The main focus of my training method is to develop players who are:
1. armed with the full repertoire of basic skills and first touch options
2. balanced physically (equally capable with both feet)
3. mentally available to envision every playing option in any game situation

I hope I've given you some food for thought the next time you sit down to take in a match, at any level. Watch the players. Watch how the game slows down and playing options are lost because of a poor or meaningless first touch. Look for "lost" opportunities due to a player being out and out one-footed. On the positive side, watch for that meaningful first touch by the midfielder that sees him clear of his marker and into open spaces at pace. Try to identify each player's dominant foot. If you find a player who makes this difficult, who seems to use both feet with equal aplomb, finding teammates with passes to all directions, you've stumbled across a rare thing indeed: **The 360° Player**.

Introduction

Are the players playing soccer in a skilful manner or are they just simply playing the game by virtue of their physical presence? - Which is which is difficult at times to recognize unless you know what to look out for. When the game of soccer is played quickly it is hard to follow the moves made by the players in detail. In other words the game can be so quick that there just simply is very little time to dwell on any one playing moment. If you are watching the game on television, sometimes the camera operators will slow the action down and you can see the details of the physical movements more clearly. The images that you see will either show quality skills on the ball or expose the lack of skills. In my coaching method I am very interested in the details of the game and whether, therefore, the players move the ball physically to the best possible result. What I would like to do here is to give you an insight into my philosophy on the way the game of soccer should be played by giving you lots of explanations on my area of interest, which is the development of the player based on what I call 'The Square On aAbility' and related soccer playing skills. One way of describing what I mean by all of that is to describe typical playing moments from any game of soccer. The practical coaching topics and examples that I will talk about, therefore, are in keeping with my philosophy. My number one opinion is that even gifted soccer players should be developed to be two footed and trained to possess a wide range of playing options. In this book you will also find an in-depth examination of the effects of the training environments that are influenced by the natural use of the right foot and therefore the consequences of that reality. You will also find solutions to the development of two footedness (the ability to control the ball skilfully with either foot) and therefore some of the more relevant skills for playing soccer.

LEGEND FOR DIAGRAMS

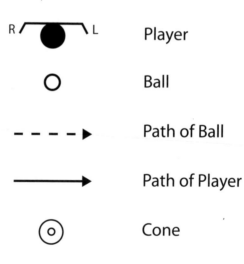

R ╱ ● ╲ L   Player

○   Ball

- - - - ▶   Path of Ball

───────▶   Path of Player

⊙   Cone

Chapter 1 – The Balanced Physical Reality

It is possible to hide the playing standards in any game of soccer. You need simply to ask the players to run like hares and battle like the wind.
No one will tell the difference. That, in my opinion, is cheating; cheating the public and, more importantly, cheating the players. The development of a soccer player is not just about running or scrapping.

The proper development of the player requires a great deal of knowledge, patience and time. Let's begin talking about the issues involved by first examining the ignorance surrounding the use of the so-called strong foot to play soccer. The out and out one footedness of the player is not a virtue, it is a problem in terms of player development and in terms of the development of much higher playing standards. My explanations will surely put the record straight.

I was watching a game of soccer and noticed that the majority of the players took lots of touches to the ball with their dominant (usually their right) foot and never once took a touch to the ball with their non-dominant (usually their left) foot. Observing what went on during the game I realized that coaches didn't say anything about how many touches a player took to the ball. They obviously did not pick up on what taking lots of touches to the ball with the so-called 'one foot' meant to not only the physical development of the player but also to the flow of the game tactically. It was obvious to me that any conditioned games of two touches to the ball on the training ground didn't filter through to the actual game of soccer. The evidence for that was everywhere to be seen on the pitch where the majority of players kept the ball with their "good" foot. The most interesting points about the above observation are the results of that observation from a coaching point of view. What I realized is that there is a difference between playing soccer and the problems of player development. In my way of thinking there are lots of things wrong with any player taking too many touches to the ball with the one foot from a development point of view. This observation is also true from a playing point of view, although I do acknowledge that there are times in the game where players will run at defenders with the ball and in that case they will obviously take lots of touches to the ball.

The most important issue here for me to begin my explanations is the fact that most players are employing just the one foot to play soccer.

In this typical game scenario player A1 is apparently doing well keeping the ball on his right foot.

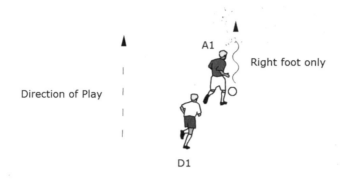

A1

Right foot only

Direction of Play

D1

Player A1 Running with the ball – Keeping the ball on the right foot down the line, with the defender chasing him.

Not That Good

It is true that coaches and players alike can get away with a lot. Unless you are an expert you won't know whether the players are delivering a good game of soccer or not. Sometimes what looks good is anything but, effective or otherwise. It is a question of assessing what is effective soccer and what is simply posturing. In the above scenario the player may look good running like a greyhound down the line until you assess the situation and realize that he may well be locked into the action by virtue of his one footedness. The player looks good and is performing to his strength but this has in effect created a set mentality that limits his options. He is likely to keep the ball on his right foot and fail to see any other playing solutions. My observations firmly point me in the direction of the reality that the game of soccer is not being played as well as it can be all over the world. In some countries the players are skilful and in other countries the players are more physical. In all cases the game is inconsistent in terms of playing standards. In my observations of the game I find a most compelling reason for the lower standards of play, namely, the lack of significant progress into the issues involved with the one footedness of the players. Developing players who are physically strong on both the right and left side of the body is the key to creating higher standards of play. The quest to develop players to be able to play the ball with either foot should be taken more seriously because it is logical to conclude that if a player is weak on one side of the body he will not be confident in the use of that side of the body.

Here is a simple test of the problem:

Coaches always rely on good evidence to convince them if something is right. I will always maintain that the balanced development of the player in terms of his strength and abilities is the key to higher standards of play.

I think you will have to concede that if a player is weak on one side of the body he will have problems in playing soccer to a high standard.

I have devised a simple test to show what a balanced player should be from a development point of view.

Note – In this format the test is based on the ability to perform the physical actions while staying 'Square On' to the ball and the line of cones. The lateral movements are performed with the inside instep of either foot to the ball with a square-on body position. The physical movements with the ball in this format are in effect the key that opens the door to the player's development in terms of his physical balance and therefore his two footed playing capability.

The Test

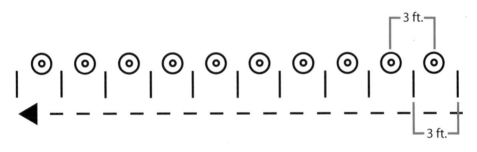

Moving Right to Left - right foot inside instep to left foot inside instep to the gaps between the cones maintaining a square-on body position

This is the lateral working format.

Note – The player will work the ball to the lateral (sideways) angle. There are serious reasons for this – explanations follow.

In the above format the test is simply based on whether the player can work the ball (sideways) down the line of cones and maintain his square-on body position.

Technically speaking - Working the ball by applying the inside instep to the ball with either foot;

Test – The Working direction is set to 'Right to left' –

Set Objective - The player will use the inside instep to move the ball to the left, playing the ball to the gaps between the cones. The right inside instep begins the movements. Player A1 moves the ball to his left on his first touch with the inside instep of the right foot to the first gap. In the next gap it is the left inside instep that stops the ball momentarily. The right foot then moves the ball on again and so on parallel with and down the line of cones. This inside instep to inside instep action is continued to the end of the line of cones as shown. The player must perform the inside instep movements with the ball with his body square-on and parallel to the line of cones.

For example - Staying Square-On

The player plays the ball sideways to each gap without turning his shoulders or his body away from the line of cones.

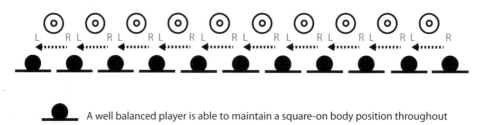

A well balanced player is able to maintain a square-on body position throughout

This diagram shows the 'Square on' shoulder position held in place during the action requested (ball skill) – The shoulder position in this configuration shows a balanced, well developed player. The shoulder position is called 'Square-on' – Being square-on to the action is a serious physical ability that matters in the game of soccer in all areas of player development. The test lies in whether the player can stay square-on to the touches on the ball while moving the ball from one inside instep to the next to the gaps in the cone placements in a rhythmic manner.

For example - Set Result - The cones are a guide to the correct physical movements with the ball.

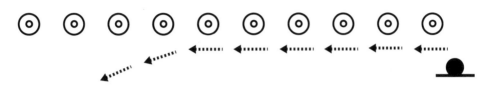

A player who is weak with his left side will fall away from the line of cones, losing his square-on body position.

Problem - If the player is weak on the left side of the body the player will simply lose his left side and turn to that side, away from the line of cones.

When the left shoulder of the player is unable to be kept in shape to the square-on body position, he will fall away to the left. This player can be said to be physically unbalanced and therefore in effect not fully developed.

The test is not just a test – I use the above format to work on the development of the player's 'Square-on ability' and its consequences which will obviously be discussed throughout this work. The main theme of my coaching philosophy is based on developing the player physically to be able to stay square on to the action as shown by example in the diagram on page 4 –I believe that the development of the square on body position results in a better – more physically balanced player. The quest to develop the more balanced player is based on working formats that are neutral. They focus on the player's development on both the right and left side of the body and therefore on the development of two footedness. I believe that if a player develops his weaker side he will make use of it during the game and the ability to use both feet to effectively play the ball gives him a true advantage in all aspects of play.

Coming Inside With The Ball

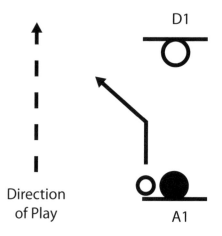

When a player is strong on his left side he will take the option of coming inside the defender, as shown by the above diagram. Being two footed gives the player a different attitude and belief in his abilities. A confident player will not hesitate to go to the right or the left of the defensive player.

Chapter 2 – The Natural Instinctive Phenomena

One of the biggest problems as far as I am concerned in terms of player development comes from the habitual effects that exist in everyday life that stem from the natural forward moving world. Many of the physical habitual effects such as walking do support the use of the right hand and consequently the use of the right foot. This is because in walking the human being does have a leading leg. The leading leg (the leg that moves forward first) can be genetically in place even before he takes a single step. It is possible to observe this when a baby first tries to walk up the stairs. Which leg will the child place on the next rung of the stairs? Will it be the left foot or the right foot? It is hard to make the connection between any genetic input and nurture because of the intervention by the mother. Some interventions (interaction between mother and child) could in effect force the child to use the right hand when he is in fact genetically programmed to use the left hand. After all, it is possible to be born right or left handed and if no one intervenes then whatever is the case will stay in place. I want to take you through the reality of our right - handed world and its consequences to the game of soccer.

The Consequences Of the Righthanded Mentality

My findings are simple enough. We need to consider just why it is that players are predominantly one footed and in the majority of players just why it is that this happens to be the right foot. I believe that the one footedness of the player is a result of thousands of years of evolution and practical every day mother to child interaction, both nurtured and genetic. That being the case, does it mean that the two footedness of the player is also a question of development?

In any event, the competence of any limb is always a question of development. The only difference between the two, whether genetic or nurtured, lies in the reality that a genetically programmed limb (neurological intervention) that does not go through any process of human intervention will obviously gain a start on the opposite limb. This means that the other limb needs to be brought back in through development. In other words, it is possible to develop any limb to a competent level.

1 – The continuous development of the muscles and therefore of any single limb will have its effect on the body. If the right hand is dominant, then it will be stronger than the left hand. If the right foot is dominant, then it will be stronger than the left foot.

2 – Continuous development of a limb, like for example the exclusive use of the one foot will have the same effect. This will make the leg stronger.

In all cases of a lack of balance (the lesser use of a particular limb) the result is seen in the development of a psychological problem, a lack of confidence in the use of a limb that is not the mainstay of any physical endeavour.

Small Steps – Big Consequences

The player development problems stem from a small beginning. The mother who hands a toy to the right hand of her baby is inadvertently promoting the use of the right hand. The effect of the use of the right hand neurologically speaking promotes the use of the right foot. Hence the right foot and the right hand (with some exceptions) dominate the physical reality of everyday endeavours. The effect of the use of the right hand and the right foot that supports the use of the right hand promotes the reality today that most soccer players are right footed. What concerns me most are the effects and therefore the implications of the right handed world on the development of soccer players. The problem with this right handed world is that it produces a weak physical side of the body which impacts on players in a negative way, especially in players who have been using one hand and one foot for a long time without redress. The problems regarding standards of play result from the reality that players are predominantly one footed. In practical terms, therefore, all problems of a physical nature result from the reality that most people are either left alone to develop naturally to be one handed and therefore one footed, or nurtured regardless of their genetics to be one handed (right hand use) or one footed (right foot in use). Most afflicted with this problem (no intervention to redress the issues of a balanced approach to the physical development) end up having no confidence in the use of one side of the body. In any event most are simply left to cope with having a weak side. The effects of this can be seen in the following examples.

While we are on the subject of the negative effects of one footedness lets also take the time to look at the positive effects of the opposite condition, 'Two Footedness', and compare the difference in the playing standards.

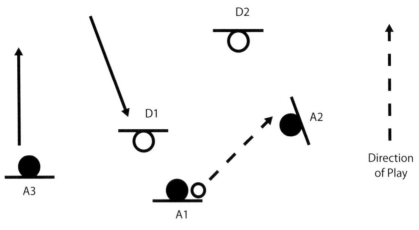

D2

D1

A2

A3

A1

Direction
of Play

Freeze Frame The Action Please

What are the implications of the 'One footedness' of a soccer player? Here are simple examples to show the effects of the forward moving world on the game of soccer. I will obviously concentrate on the problems associated with one footedness and how it reduces the playing options. In other examples on this issue we will discuss the benefits of a two-footed capability and how this impacts on the game of soccer. Here are a few examples of playing moments that can in effect result in either higher standards of play or lower standards of play.

What is going on in the above example explains the problem associated with one footedness. The game of soccer is a quick game today. It is athletic, fast and physical. When it is played in a competitive manner, players must make quick decisions to solve different playing problems. If a player is not developed properly he will simply react naturally to any event. When a player who is not developed properly finds himself in the above game scenario, what will he do? He will do what comes naturally. That is often the problem. Doing things naturally doesn't always mean doing things well. If the player is not developed properly and is out and out one footed, he will be weak on the left side of his body and strong and confident in the use of the right side of the body. His reaction will be instinctive and as a result the playing options will be limited.

Consequently - As shown by the above example; – When the defender D1 comes to challenge Player A1 – Player A1 in possession of the ball will naturally move the ball to his strong side. The first reaction of players who are one footed will be to move the ball to the strong side, which is the right foot in the above example – The player will be said to be playing to his strength. In truth he will in fact be playing to his weakness. Looking at the diagram, it is clear that one very viable playing option is a pass to player A3, but if player

A1 is indeed an out and out right footer, this option will not be an option at all because he will instinctively look only to move the ball to the right of the defender. Are such issues significant? Of course! If the defensive players (opponents) dictate what happens during the game, that's a problem from a playing standards point of view. This is because higher playing standards depend on how the player in possession of the ball solves the playing problems. They depend on;

1 –The physical capability of the player in possession of the ball.

2 – Fast thinking solutions that will deal with the physical presence of the opponent that will try to dictate what happens within the game of soccer.

It is simply true to say that if in the attacking phase of the game the defensive players dictate play, it indicates a number of problems.

1 – The players may lack the physical balance to play soccer effectively.

2 – The players may not be skilful enough to solve the problems posed by their opponent.

The above points of reference spell a lower standard of play. Teams that have little or no skills on the ball will end up defending for all they are worth. The lack of goals in a game of soccer can tell you a lot about the players. If the defense dictates what happens to the ball, the game of soccer becomes negative from a goal scoring point of view and the quality of the game in terms of the overall playing standards is not very good. It is not good for the image of the game to have a 0-0 draw. Most supporters of the game of soccer today want to watch a positive game of soccer where they can see goals being created and scored. The problem is that the more creative type of game requires the players to be unpredictable, skilful, fast and yet strong and graceful. That type of game requires more players on the field of play to actually be able to play the ball with either foot, to be two footed.

For Example -

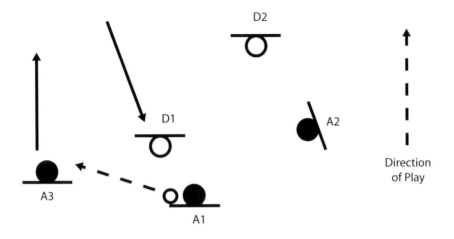

Higher Standards Of Play
The Difference In Playing Standards

Note - The difference in playing standards comes from the ability of the player to play the ball with either the left or the right foot.
If the player is two footed (able to play the ball with either foot) he can change his mind and affect more readily whatever playing option he wants.

In the above example player A1 is capable of playing the ball with either foot. When player A1 is two footed as is shown by the above example, it is certainly a much harder deal for any defensive player. In this example defender D1 will not affect what A1 will want to do in terms of his attacking playing options. The two footedness of the player will obviously give him more options and therefore more attacking solutions. It is logical to conclude that if the player has more than one playing solution his actions will be more unpredictable and therefore more difficult for the defense to deal with and ultimately more exciting to watch. These are important reasons why we should be concerned about any player that will only use his "strong" foot to play the ball.

Chapter 3 – The Lateral Format Training Environment

Should the 'Coaches' of soccer players understand the difference between all development environments whether it's the home or school or even at the soccer club in terms of their effects on a player's development?
The short answer to that is - Yes! Every development environment without exception has its consequences to the development of a player. In all their differences there is an overriding factor that I believe has contributed to the downfall of many a good coaching concept. In this chapter I will endeavour to explain what that overriding factor is and just why this factor has impacted negatively on players' progress.

The Forward Moving Game

It is said that the game of soccer is a forward moving game. That statement only tells part of the story. There are other statements too that are just as important to the development concerns of soccer players. The problems of a physical and technical development nature to play effective soccer that can affect any player don't just begin at the soccer club. The difficulties emerge with the reality that the physical development of all concerned is geared up to the natural forward moving angle and that this supports the natural physical side of any human being. In truth the problems associated with player development concerns such as the lack of ability to play effective soccer begin with the reality that all children develop natural skills, such as walking, jogging and running and sprinting, long before they take up the game of soccer seriously. Question is, just why would such natural forward moving skills like walking spell trouble in terms of the development of the player? The number one reason that such skills create the environment for a lack of progress in the player's ability to play effective soccer comes from the fact that such human skills as walking are strictly forward moving, whereas the game of soccer is made up of lots of different physical movements in every direction and do not always conform to the principles of the natural forward moving world.

Problems - The trouble in terms of a lack of progress in the development of the player begins when the principles of the forward moving game come into conflict with the obstacles found on the soccer pitch, namely the opponent. The opponent in effect creates a barrier in the forward direction, impeding an offensive player's movement in that direction. This "barrier" is in the way of the player's primary objective, which is the creation and scoring of a goal.

The direct line to goal can be blocked by defenders. You obviously can't go through them, so what can you do? Go around them, of course! But how do you do that from a soccer playing point of view? You can apply different one on one skills like the skill of **moving the ball off the line**.

The Lateral Angle – This touch can be played to the left or right of the player.

The trouble from a development point of view comes from the reality that you can't always move forward with the ball. When you come up against a defensive position you have to have the right skills to deal with that reality. There are skills that player A1 will apply to some situations during play that are not forward moving. The skill of moving the ball off the line is a skill that is not a forward moving skill and cannot therefore be performed by a player who can only move the ball with the right foot to a forward moving direction. The skill of moving the ball off the line is a skill that is played to the lateral angle. It's a skill that requires lateral strength and therefore the 'lateral' physical ability to apply the right and the left foot to the movements involved in the creation of this skill. In terms of playing angles therefore it is better to say that the game of soccer is made up of (from a player development point of view) two major angles of play.

1 – The forward moving angle – Natural

2 – The lateral working angle – Requires development

First Things First

Let's get back to basics; All of the skills mentioned and the ones that we will look at later require the player to be two footed and to possess the physical square-on ability. The above reference points 1 and 2 form part of the solution to the square-on ability and to the two footedness of the player. Knowing the function of the square-on ability and how to develop it is important.

The Left Foot Drag Back Skill

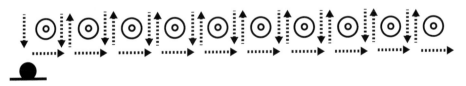

Left foot drag back. Left foot inside instep. Right foot forward touch. Repeat.

14

If a player is weak on the left side of the body, he should work the drag back skill from left to right in the above format. The drag back of the ball with the underside of the left boot is repeated in the following working sequence: Left foot drags the ball back from the back of the line of cones to the side of player A1. From that point in the action the ball is moved to the right with the inside instep of the left foot. That makes it two touches to the ball with the left foot so far. The right foot is then applied to move the ball forward and through the gap to the back of the line of cones. At that point in the movement the player drags the ball back again to his side of the line with the underside of his left boot. All of the movements should flow without a pause in the action. No stopping and starting again, just keep going. Keep repeating the working sequence given down the line of cones where the drag back of the ball becomes the main theme of the practice. This action with the ball strengthens the left side of the player through an effect known as kinetic tension and also through the fact that the player will repeat the movements favoring his left foot/leg to a set working sequence that is guided by the cone placements. There are nine cone placements. The working sequence is set to a 2:1 ratio - 2 touches with the left foot – 1 touch with the right foot.

The Right Foot Drag Back Skill

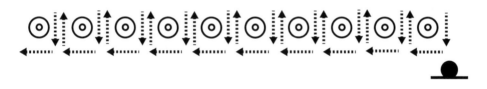

Right foot drag back. Right foot inside instep Left foot forward touch. Repeat.

If the right foot is weak, the player starts from the right of the format as we look. The sequence of work is the same as described previously but naturally the theme of the practice centers on the right foot, which again performs the touches to a ratio of work; 2 touches with the right foot and 1 touch with the left foot. The same movements are repeated to every gap time and time again until there are no gaps left in the line of cones. Repeating the movements with the right foot would make it 20 touches with the right foot and 9 with the left foot.

The Square-On Physical Ability

Try to make sure that the physical balance is always in place and that the player is therefore equally strong on both sides of his body. If the player is not strong equally on both sides of the body then logical intervention is necessary.

The obvious signs to see if that's the case is the ability of the player to move the ball to the working pattern equally well with the right or left foot. If the player can do that he is physically balanced and can be said to possess the square-on ability. If the player is weak on one side, focus the work on that side to its logical conclusion. When the player is strong and equally good with either foot he will have more playing options. It is true to say that players who have the square-on ability can do more with the ball than players who do not.

When under pressure they can pass the ball to a 180° angle without any problems.

For Example

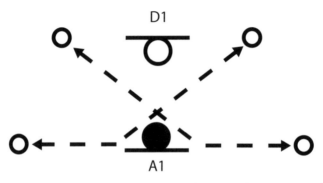

They can play the pass to any direction with the right foot or the left foot, no problem. They can also stay square-on to the direction of the attacking play and apply the right or the left foot to pass the ball to the 180° angle. No problem.

Right Or Left

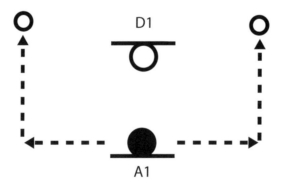

When put under pressure - They can go past any defensive position to the right or left of any defensive player – Player A1 can go past the defender D1 to the left or right side. In that case the defensive player can't put the attacking player on his weak foot because player A1 hasn't got a weak side/foot.

Finishing/scoring goals.

Great scorers can score with either foot. How many times have you seen a player struggle to score a goal because the ball came to his so-called weak foot and he either swung and missed or skewed the ball to the corner flag rather than into the opponent's goal? This would not happen if the player was equally good with both feet.

When scoring goals - They can strike the ball with the right or left foot – It shouldn't be a problem – The player should be able to strike the ball from any angle.

The above are all simple examples of what the player SHOULD be able to do with either foot. The square-on body position and therefore the ability of the player to play the ball with either foot is a serious issue. Every professional soccer player should be able to play the ball with either foot.
If the player will not be able to play the ball with either foot then he will not be able to perform at least half the skills on show. Why at least half? It's logical to conclude that if the player is only able to use the left or the right foot he won't be able to perform all the skills and therefore effectively work to all the angles of play available to him in any given situation on the soccer pitch. The square-on ability and therefore the two footedness of the player is vital. The skills on show adhere to the lateral development angle and of course to the natural forward moving angle as well. The forward moving angle adheres to the natural endeavours such as running, while the lateral angle adheres to the development of one on one skills (going past opponents) – and of course to many other soccer playing skills such as the first touch options. For example, 'The Extended Touch', which we will take a look at in the appropriate chapter later.

Examine the skill of 'Moving the ball off the line'. This touch on the ball is a very useful skill to have because it allows the player to change the angle of play in relation to either the opponent who is blocking the way forward or an oncoming challenger who wants to get to the ball. This touch is one of the more effective touches on the ball when you want to keep possession. Moving the ball off the line and the ability to play that touch option with either foot makes it possible to keep the ball in a tight area of play.

For Example

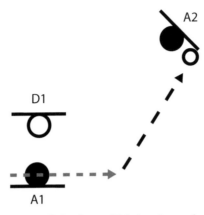

Player A1 – Moving the ball off the line - This is a lateral angle touch option –

In the above example player A1 uses the inside instep of the left foot to move the ball off the line on his right shoulder and open up the angle of play to his right hand side. This touch takes the ball away from the defensive player D1 – The two footedness of the player here enables him to apply the touch to the ball that moves the ball to the side with his left foot (left to right) and make the pass with the right foot to player A2.

The solution to the many different playing problems often requires different playing skills. Some physical interpretations of playing solutions can even be much more complicated in terms of the physical performance. The following example explains what I mean.

For Example

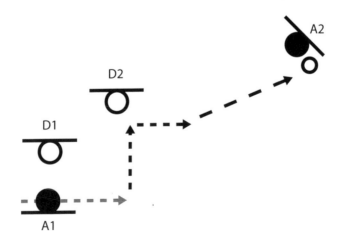

Two footed. Left foot – right foot – left foot – pass with the right foot – ball touch combination.

Player A1 moves the ball off the line with the inside instep of the left foot, leaving the defensive player D1 to his left side, then takes another touch to the ball, this time forward of the first challenger with the right foot and then the left foot inside instep moves the ball off the line again to avoid D2 (Cover) and the right foot then passes the ball to player A2.

It is important to appreciate that in practical terms most of the specialized skills of soccer require a completely different approach from a physical development point of view to that of any natural physical forward moving endeavour. From a player development point of view there are issues involving the forward moving world that cannot be ignored. The forward moving world is effective in the promotion of the one footedness of the player and its consequences.

In combination, forward movement and lateral movement solve many of the development problems associated with soccer players and their quest to develop exceptional playing qualities. The lateral working formats are essential to the development of the player's two footedness because they address the requirements for physical balance.

As illustrated earlier, the correctly developed player will stay square on to the action. To clarify, here it is again:

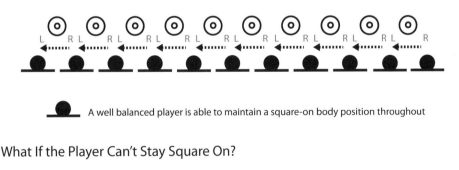

A well balanced player is able to maintain a square-on body position throughout

What If the Player Can't Stay Square On?

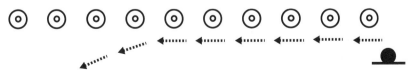

A player who is weak with his left side will fall away from the line of cones, losing his square-on body position.

In this diagram the player is weak on the left side of his body. How do I know that? When he moves the ball right to left in this format he is not able to stay square on when moving the ball with the inside instep of either foot, from gap to gap, parallel to the line of cones, right to left. In the above example the player could not move the ball from gap to gap because he wasn't strong enough on the left side of the body. The right side of his body was simply too strong for the left side and he collapsed, or gave way if you prefer, on his left side in favor of the stronger right side. Hence his left shoulder turned away from the square on position.

Note – In the first diagram, the player is balanced. He is strong on both the right and left side.

A strong purpose - It is important to understand that the weak side of the player is a problem and not a virtue. If the player can't stay square on he will not be able to play the ball to every direction possible and more importantly he will not be able to use the weak side of the body to any good effect. So, in the strong left footed player we need to obviously work on the development of the right side of his body and in the strong right sided player we need to work on the left side. In cases where the player is out and out right footed you would have to spend a fair amount of time addressing his physical balance.

It is also important to note that in addressing the balance you do not destroy the natural talent of the player. On the contrary you in effect enhance the ability of the player because in strengthening his weak side you improve his physical balance and enable him to move the ball effectively to any direction of play.

Chapter 4 – Playing To Their Strength

Whatever the arguments, it seems to me that unless human behavior changes somewhat, one fact of life will exist forever and a day: most people end up being right handed. When a mother has a baby she doesn't go into the genetic make up of the child. Whether the child is right or left handed won't matter to her. If she is right handed she will develop the baby's right hand and that's that. In some places in the world the use of the right hand is set in stone so to speak.

There are lots of different interventions into every child's development by the adult world that everyone or nearly everyone will conform to and there is no getting away from that. Whether we agree on all issues or not I am sure that you will agree with me on the following points of reference. The coaching methods should at least have the following objectives;

1 – Develop the physical body to be strong and capable of playing soccer in a way that's fully functional.

2 – Develop the physical body in a way that facilitates the use of both feet while playing soccer

Explaining 1 – To function fully in a way that's beneficial to the game of soccer means to be balanced physically in terms of strength on both the right and left side of the body. This is essential to the performance of many of the movements performed with or without the ball that make up the game of soccer.

Explaining 2 - The physical development of the player should be done in a way that enables him to build a repertoire of soccer skills that will allow him to perform the skills of soccer physically, technically and with the right attitude mentally with the right and/or left side of the body.

The Forward Moving Training World

If we agree to any of the above, then like me you will find it odd that the training of soccer players is something that has only been taken seriously for the last fifteen years or so. That's not to say that soccer players of the past didn't train hard. It is simply an observation of **HOW** they trained. There is a misunderstanding here of immense implications to the game of soccer and to the development of the players themselves. What I have found is that most training sessions are at what I call 'The Next Level of Soccer' – that is, they simply apply training formats that assume many, many things about the players, especially in the professional ranks. After all, who would question players like Ronaldo for example. It is simply taken for granted that a player of this calibre can play soccer, that he can kick the ball properly, pass the ball properly, play a one on one skill properly, etc. In other words, if the player is in the first team then it is taken for granted that he can play soccer. That's very interesting to me. What I have seen for years is that they in many respects (no disrespect to anyone intended here) have put the horse before the cart without realizing it. The training grounds are often simply geared up for group work where the practicing endeavours are obvious playing moments like crossing the ball into the penalty area and finishing (getting on the end of crosses and scoring goals). In essence, "Playing soccer". All of which is fine but it does not focus on the needs of any individual player. "Rubbish!" you say? Again I hope you will allow me to explain further.

The training environment has been greatly simplified as a result of accepting players the way they are. The message is that players don't need coaching, they just need to play soccer. That is what I am referring to when I say the horse was put before the cart. Especially at the upper levels, it is more often than not taken for granted that a player can either play soccer or he cannot. I suppose this makes sense somewhat when you prescribe to the premise that if a player is good enough to become a professional then he must know everything. Who would dare to question the abilities of a player being paid a hundred thousand pounds sterling per week? I would, for one. I would because I know that the training environments out there don't question the players enough in respect to their true concerns. I maintain that a lot of top class players could be even better if they were aware of and addressed their own personal weaknesses.

Inherent Realities

The lack of attention paid to the implications of the forward moving world, some of which I have already mentioned, is alarming.

Most training sessions cater in practical terms to the strong side of the players, virtually ignoring their "weak" side. This kind of simplification of the training and playing domain does not encourage skill development, in fact it inhibits it. In this simplified set-up, players rely on high fitness levels to give them the chance to win, not on the skills side of the game.

What do I mean by the "simplification of the training domain"? In the following example the face of the clock explains the implications. Because the majority of players are right footed, play tends to move in a counter-clockwise direction (to the right). Many a left footed player will tell you that they hardly got a look in at some clubs where everything is geared up for the right footers' needs.

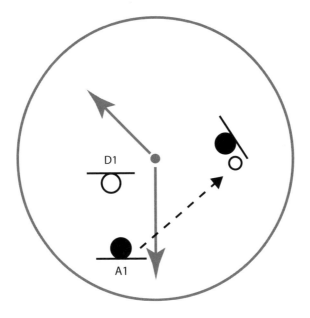

The Left Footers

It is strange that in some ways the left footers will benefit from the counter clockwise domain because they are in effect working on their weak side, the right foot.

In all other respects 'The counter-clockwise training directions' that favor the right footers are significant to the game of soccer in a number of serious ways. The consequences of the right foot playing preference is the effect that most players naturally discard the clockwise direction and therefore the playing options that exist on the left side of the clock. The implications of this are that within lower standards of play and indeed even in so-called higher standards of play there is a natural tendency to have some games being played more on the right side of the pitch than on the left. The result is a lack balance in terms of attacking play. I have seen games of soccer where you can have a picnic on the left side of the pitch and no one would know you were there. The left side of the soccer pitch is not the natural playing domain for any out and out right footed player.

From the practice ground to the practical playing experience –

When under pressure (challenged) the natural instincts make the player A1 move the ball to his strong side. In practical terms, therefore, when the opponent D1 challenges player A1 for possession of the ball, the right footed player A1 will naturally move the ball on to his strong side. The development of the player in the 'Counter clockwise' training environment has made this the norm. In many training sessions the weak side of the player has simply ended up being left out of the working equation. The right foot of the player is worked on every day while the weak (left) side is left to its own conclusions. Some coaches realizing the problem recently have made efforts to address this issue. The trouble is that unless you get away from the counter clockwise working domain and the school environment and the mother's input, etc. , you won't address the issues properly and you will simply continue to enforce the use of the one good foot. In places like England, where the competition for professional contracts is fierce and where the game is more and more commercially orientated, the out and out one footed player is not good enough for the top end of the professional game. Young players should be taught the value of two footedness and indeed devote their time to the practice of becoming two footed. Given the right approach to training there is every chance of achieving any objective. Let's examine further some of the more relevant issues and indeed the solutions to development of soccer skills. It is important to implement working formats that actually deal with the problems associated with the two sides of the game:

1 – The Defense – Stopping the opponent from scoring more goals than your own team.

2 – The Attack – Scoring more goals than the opponents.

I would have to say that the worst thing that could have happened to the game of soccer over the last twenty or so years has happened. Namely, the use of playing solutions that have simply catered for the strong side of the player while ignoring his weaknesses. These playing solutions include conditioning the game to two touches of the ball, running with the ball as a sole means of playing in the final third of the pitch, keeping the ball for the sake of possession, and kicking the ball long from defense, missing the midfield out as if they were not part of the team from an attacking point of view. These practices have in effect stymied the development of skilful and creative players, and instead placed more importance on the physical qualities of the players, namely size and strength. Players are being selected, not for their skills but for their hardness in the tackle. All of this has created a negative game of soccer, not a great game of soccer.

Why? Because when players are asked to take two touches to the ball, for example, they lose the reality of what the skills of soccer are from a movement point of view and from a playing point of view. When the long ball over the midfield is the play of choice, midfielders no longer require skills on the ball, they merely need to be able to defend when the opponent wins the ball and counter attacks. It is a vicious circle: the lack of skills leads to practices that lead to a lack of skills. This is a serious point because in effect when you condition the game of soccer to two touches or the like – Long ball etc - every player in the practice mode adapts physically to the needs of the game. If the needs are simplified, the physical development adapts to the simplification of the physical movements and the players are lesser players for it, that's the simple truth. That's the big issue.

Chapter 5 – The Two Footedness Capability

Most of us accept that in all other professions you have to work on your skills. The game of soccer is no different. There are soccer skills that are not fancy footwork but are simply basic to the game of soccer. The square on ability, for example, is basic to the game of soccer, which is why it is a physical ability that has to be developed. The square on position allows the player to play the ball to any direction he wishes, using either the left or right foot. I hope that all of this is clear.

The Square On Ability

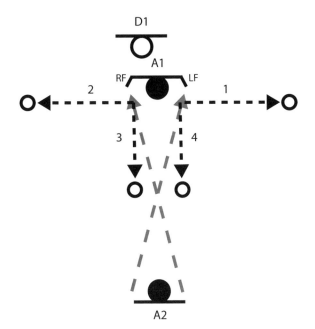

From a first touch options perspective - In the above example player A1 demonstrates the importance of developing the 'Square On' ability.
In this typical playing scenario we have a defensive player goal side and to the back of the attacking player A1. Player A1 in this example has his back to the opponent D1. This demonstrates some of the reasons for the development of the square on ability and therefore the need to develop the two footedness of the player. When the player is strong on both sides he can develop a wide range of playing solutions. Player A1 can play the ball to more angles and therefore keep the ball away from the opponent.

Touch Development

When the player can stay square on because he is strong on both the right and left side, he can take a better touch to the ball. A good repertoire of first touch options makes all the difference. In the above example player A1 Is demonstrating his touch options against the defensive player D1.

1 – The right foot inside instep touch – takes the ball to the player's left.
4 – The left foot inside instep touch – takes the ball forward
2 – The left foot inside instep touch – takes the ball to the player's right.
3 – The right foot inside instep touch – takes the ball forward

In recent years, especially in England, coaches have become content with prescribing blanket solutions to playing problems. These blanket solutions, in whatever form they take, can only be called conditioned games of soccer. They as a form of development are not good. The worst of conditioned games of soccer can only be described as spoilers of the game. When the spoilers are used such as 'Kick the ball high into the air', 'Play the ball long' or 'Run with the ball in the final third', no matter what other options may exist, the development of players is stifled. The game of soccer should not employ blanket solutions to everything. There are moments in the game when the pass is a priority. When taking someone on is a priority. When shielding the ball away from the defender is a priority. When playing the long ball is a priority. When dribbling with the ball against more than one defensive player is a priority. When striking the ball in an effort to score a goal is a priority. The players on the pitch should have the ability and the permission to decide what to do in any game situation. Conditioning players to do certain things in certain playing situations is simply the wrong way of developing any player.

Here is a simple reality check on the bad solutions that have crept into the game in the last fifteen or so years.

Note - There is a time in the game for any of the following playing options. However, some managers have made their players play to them throughout the game. The game of soccer should be played to a wide range of skills. Simply conditioning the players to keep doing the same thing over and over again is wrong from a player development point of view.

Questionable Playing Solutions:

1 – Kick the ball high up into the air at every opportunity

Note - This will definitely have an effect on the game. It's a tactic used when a team is playing a better class of opposition. The game is ruined because if the ball is high up in the air no one can get hold of it. Quite obviously, the benefit to the players is limited!

2 – Play the ball long

Note - There are times when this is the correct solution, but when players are told to do so every time they get the ball in defense they will never gain the necessary tactical understanding or skills to be great. Telling players that there is only one tactical option in any situation is harmful to their development. The benefit to the players is limited!

3 - Keeping the ball

There is a time for everything in the game of soccer and keeping the ball to take the last man on in defense is one of them. It is of course possible for any strong/right/left footed player to play soccer by taking lots of touches to the ball (keeping the ball) and going on a dribbling run – However, keeping the ball without considering other playing options (players in a better position perhaps) allows defensive players time to get behind the ball, which does not help the attacking side of the game. Keeping the ball looks good but if it is done as a blanket solution it leads to bad habits like keeping the head down and not seeing more of the playing possibilities. Such habits certainly contribute to bad play.
The benefit to the players is limited!

4 - Condition the game of soccer

Conditioned games of soccer (forcing players to play one, two or any number of touches) as a means of development definitely lead to a lack of playing skills. When players lack playing skills they rely on improvisation. Improvisation in turn leads to more touches of the ball. Lots of touches to the ball ensure the failure of the player to actually develop a wide range of effective soccer skills. The benefit to the players is limited!

In other words – It's not fair really because you wont find many players that will question their manager. If the manager wants his players to play in any of the above styles most players will conform. The benefit to the players is limited.

The only reason anyone would condition players to play in any of the above styles is to mold the player into a conformity that keeps the manager in control. That's an interesting issue. It is nothing to do with anything personal. Many of the above conditions do in fact serve a purpose. That purpose has nothing to do with player empowerment but everything to do with keeping the 'Status Quo'. We don't live in an ideal world, there are reasons why some managers would want players to play in any of the above styles. I have mentioned one of them previously which is to do with beliefs. If any manager thinks his players have no chance of winning the game against a stronger opponent he might resort to one of the above styles in the hope that it might get him a result.

Shaping Up

When a player is strong on both sides of his/her physical being and is capable of playing the ball with either foot, body position can be applied to good effect. The player can face any direction of play. That fact alone is naturally important. In playing terms the position of the body 'Is' very important. In soccer terms its called 'Shaping up'.

Shaping up – Without the ability to shape up properly the player could not take a decent touch to the ball. Playing the pass on first contact with the ball – Taking a first touch to change the direction of play - Such playing skills can only be done effectively if the player knows how to shape his body up to the ball. The body position is vital from a ball control point of view in terms of the quality of the work. The shape of the body can be used effectively in any number of ways.

Quality touches on the ball come from 'Shaping the body' to take the touch. This is because the shape of the body must support the most important part of the foot in making a soccer move. The part of the foot that takes control of the ball most effectively is the inside instep. This will never change. Yes! Of course it is possible to take a touch to the ball with the outside of the boot and even with any part of the body, save the hands. Nonetheless, the most effective touch to the ball is with the inside instep of the foot. The positioning of the body to accommodate that part of the boot to the ball is an important issue.

Shape up - For Example

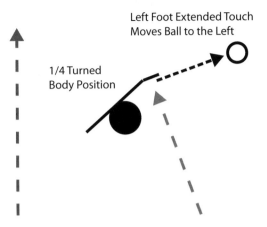

Left Foot Extended Touch
Moves Ball to the Left

1/4 Turned
Body Position

Another Example

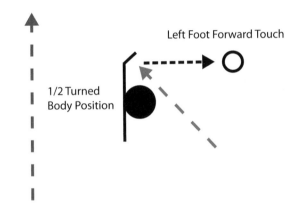

Left Foot Forward Touch

1/2 Turned
Body Position

Note – Taking the first touch to the ball in terms of keeping the ball is different to that of passing the ball on first contact with the ball. I will deal with that subject when we take a look at the pass and move training session.

I could draw you more diagrams, because there are lots of angles that each player can face. The body position is more fluent than anything I can show you here. However, shaping up to a pass or making sure that you return an accurate pass does depend on how the receiving player shapes up to the ball. The more accurate passes and indeed first touches are made with the inside instep of the boot/foot.

The secret of good ball control is to always try to position the body in such a way that the ball is taken up by the inside instep of the back foot. That's the inside instep foot position furthest away from the passer. In the above example we don't see the man making the pass, we only see the arrow showing the ball coming to the player. The successful touch on the ball – The accurate pass, depends on the position of the body which in turn sets the inside instep of the foot up to the ball. This foot position enables the player to take a decent touch or to position the ball to the angle of his choice for his next play option.

Format 1 – Shaping Up – To 'PASS' THE BALL

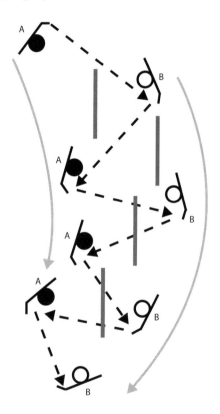

Count the body positions for the left foot inside instep pass positions – Count the body positions for the right foot inside instep pass positions.

Shape Up - The duration of the practice in this type of format is up to the coach. Players can take over at one end and rotate through the format taking turns.

In the above example the ball is 'worked' around and between the sticks using 1-2s. Start at the far end; The left foot pass made by the inside instep of player A begins the working sequence. Pass one stick placement = one pass – Pass between the two sticks = two passes – Moving on, pass to the outside of the second stick = third pass and so on, to the end of the format.

Work the ball one way, past all the sticks, then back again, past the sticks, playing the ball on first contact. No extra touches on the ball.

Players shape up to each pass moving down the format, working the pass to the correct foot. At some point the players can do a double take. In other words, the pass is made, the ball is returned on first contact where the players don't move but double pass the ball to each other before moving on to the next stick placement.

Sometimes players pass with the right foot inside instep to the right foot inside instep of the other player. Sometimes a cross over pass is made, for example – the right foot passes the ball to the working partner's left foot.

At the start of the working sequence player A plays the ball to the left foot of player B. That's playing the pass to the inside of the player. Playing the ball to the inside of the player is playing the ball to the foot that is going to take up the ball with the inside instep. In other words, the pass is made to the foot furthest from the passer.

There are good reasons for playing the ball to the inside of the player. If you play the ball to the right foot and miss the player on the outside, the ball is gone and the player can't do anything about it. Playing the ball accurately to the inside of the player is the safer pass option. Here the player has the best chance of taking control of the ball with the biggest possible area – namely, the inside instep of the left foot. Practice shaping up to the pass and pass back.

Shaping Up – To the 'Touch'

Receiving the ball and passing the ball on and taking the first touch to the ball are not the same thing. What is a touch to the ball? Is it the one that comes at the point of contact with the ball? It can be. However, let's make a distinction here between a meaningful touch on the ball and a 'non meaningful' touch on the ball.

For Example

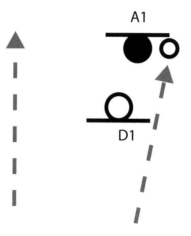

Diagram - Player A1 has taken a touch that simply stops the ball.

Is that a touch? Yes! But it's not a good touch. In all other playing scenarios it would be better if the player took a meaningful touch to the ball. It would also be better if he shaped up correctly to the touch and took the touch to a meaningful length of touch in a meaningful direction.

For example

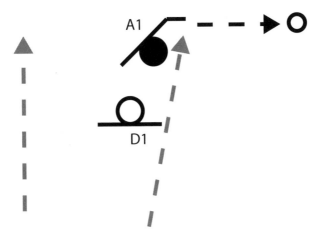

Wherever possible the player should shape up to the direction he is playing to because that helps him to take a meaningful touch to the ball with the inside instep of the foot. Taking a meaningful touch makes it easier to move the ball in the attacking direction.

We have established that the mainstay of the game of soccer is the inside instep of the foot when it comes to touch options and certain short pass options. There are other issues though. The pass can be played on first contact, as can a first touch option (described later). The first touch option and the pass option can also be played when the player is forward moving. In other words, both the touch on the ball and the pass of the ball can be played after the player has possession of the ball. That's interesting from a development point of view. Why? Because you can practice the different first touch options in their own right, just like you can practice the pass options in their own right. Here are further examples of that, keeping in mind that we are also looking at the shape up of the body to not only the practice of the different touch options but also the pass itself.

Shape up -

One of the most important touch options available to the player is the touch that 'Moves the ball off the line' This touch is played with the inside instep and can be played in any direction. It is a square on body position touch and obviously the body can face any direction the player wishes. When it comes to the development of this touch, it's the easiest in the world to organize. When it comes to playing soccer it's without a doubt the most effective touch option.

The Practice Format

Nothing could be simpler – Set two cones approximately 2.5 yards apart. Position the player in the middle and behind the two cones.

Play the pass to the player –

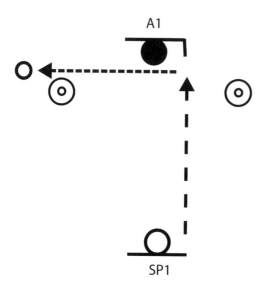

Left inside instep moves the ball to the right and left leg follows.

SP1 Plays the ball to the left foot of player A1 – A1 takes the inside instep of the left foot to the ball, keeping square on, and moves the ball to his right. This touch is taken across the body to effect the touch called 'Moving the ball off the line'. The ball is taken across the body with the inside instep of the left foot to a length of touch that is approx 1.5 yds. This length of touch and the physical movement of the leg that simply follows the touch will place the player in contact with the ball and, therefore, in control of the ball.

Square On – Shape up.

SP1 plays the ball to the inside instep of the right foot of player A1. Player A1 takes the inside instep of the right foot and moves the ball on to his left. The foot follows the touch, moving the foot and ball across his body.

We have come a long way from the conditioned game of soccer. If you can pass the ball properly and you know the off the line touch then you're in with a shout. This soccer world is not about conditioning the players to play soccer, it is about empowering the player to play soccer by giving him the skills to play soccer. In effect, we are acknowledging certain realities.

1 – Soccer skills have a structure, a physical structure that has a specific playing effect. In terms of player development the player doesn't have to rely on improvisation. He can learn how to play lots of soccer skills that are practical, useful and more importantly ones that can be worked on and improved everyday. You can't forget skills that you can practice on a regular basis, especially when the practice formats can be set up any time, almost anywhere, on any park or soccer pitch. You don't need a lot of equipment to get started working on a skill like passing and moving the ball off the line. Already we have the making of a training session.

For example; Practice Taking A Touch & Passing The Ball

The practice of the pass and shaping up to pass was done earlier. The same is true with the touch option applied in this keep ball format.

In this next example we can use the skills we already know to practice keeping the ball against a defensive player.

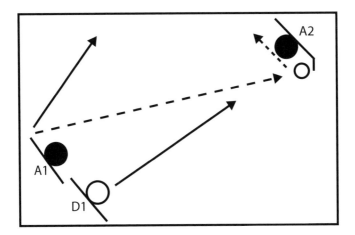

Any suitable playing area –

Bring the pass and the touch option into the above area of practice and the players have enough skills in their locker to work on keeping the ball in a fairly tight area of play. The theme of the above possession format would be to keep the ball by applying the 'off the line' touch and passing.

For the practice to work – Position the players as shown. Players A1 & B1 work together to keep the ball away from the defensive player D1.
Player A1 starts the passing sequence by playing the ball to his partner B1.
Player D1 defends. (This is hard work for D1!)

Focus here should be on the receiving player correctly shaping his body to allow him to make his 'off the line' touch in the proper direction (this depends on the position of D1 at all times). This is possible thanks to the work already done on staying square on and receiving and moving the ball with either foot. If the players aren't capable of playing the ball with either foot, they will not be able to keep the ball moving from player to player for very long in the above format. In fact, without the skill of moving the ball off line they would be lucky to get three passes in before the defender gets to the ball. For the above format to work players have to be two footed and be able to take the first touch option to the ball with the inside instep of either foot to move the ball to the lateral angle shown. At times a player may even double back on the lateral touch (play the touch one way then change and go the other way in quick succession). Higher standards of play depend on the two footedness of the player and his knowledge of the touch options on offer. Shaping up to the touch and taking the touch are not options in the above format, they are necessary skills to achieve success.

Shaping Up

Keeping the ball against a defender is one thing, but there are also moments in the game where a defender can get close enough where he can put pressure on the player with the ball. In order to keep the ball in such situations the player needs to have skills that will help him to cope with that. The skill in this next example that will help the player keep the ball in such a situation is called the 'Change Of Angle With Depth Touch', or 'Depth Touch' for short.

Here's how it works;
'Depth Touch'

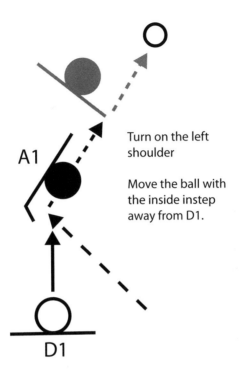

A1

Turn on the left shoulder

Move the ball with the inside instep away from D1.

D1

In this example, the defender (D1) timed his run to coincide with the ball about to reach the feet of player A1. D1 just about got to the ball, but not quite. At the last second player A1 shaped up to the ¼ body turn position, took a right foot inside instep touch to the ball and pulled the ball on the turn to his left shoulder – Turned and moved away with the ball – Simple but effective. It is relatively easy to work on such a skill. Once again the player needs to develop this touch on the left and right side of the body.

The Practice Format – Shape Up For the Depth Touch Option

Note the additional cone placement! What is it for? The angle of the touch is guided by the additional cone placement. When the player takes a touch to the ball, the touch will not be played to the square on angle. A1 will now assume a ¼ body turn to shape up to the touch angle as he takes the ball up on the inside instep of the right foot in this example. The cone to the back of the original two cone placements is a guide to the length of touch and direction of touch.

For Example – The Three Cone Placement

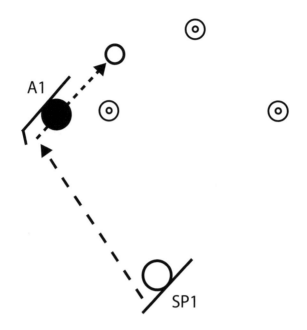

Practice pulling the ball back and turning with the ball - SP1 plays the ball to the inside instep of the right foot of player A1. A1 pulls the ball across his body with his right foot and the right foot follows the ball. In taking the depth touch from this quarter turned position A1 can turn around and shield the ball from D1 or even pull the ball back to create the space for a forward pass beyond D1.

For Example – Shape Up On The Left Foot

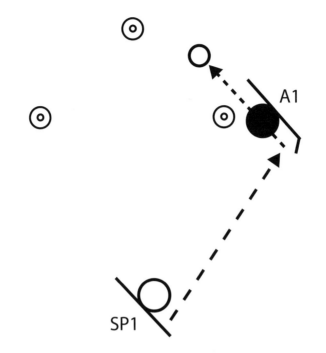

Note - In The Interest Of Balance - Each working format enables the player to work on his right and left foot capability, developing two footedness. Make sure that the player spends an equal amount of time on each side of the format.

SP1 plays the ball to the inside instep of A1's left foot. A1 assumes a quarter body turn position and moves the ball across his body with the left foot to the angle set by the back cone, turning on the touch.

The quarter body turn position enables the player to see forward of his position so it's also a good way of taking up the ball on the turn. It is also possible to turn around off a square on body position. In the following examples A1 practices taking a reverse touch option and turns around with the ball.

1 - IN PRACTICE MODE
Take a touch and shield the ball

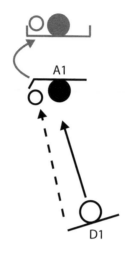

How it works – SP1 becomes D1 – When SP1 passes the ball to player A1 he follows his pass and puts pressure on the player. Player A1 takes the touch, turns and shields the ball from D1 (formerly SP1).

2 – IN PRACTICE MODE

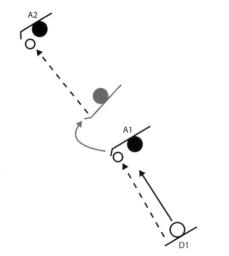

Player A1 Takes the touch – Turns and passes the ball to player A2

3 – IN PRACTICE MODE
PLAY THE BALL BEYOND THE CHALLENGER

In this touch mode the player never turns his back to the touch of the ball but stays facing his adversary (D1)

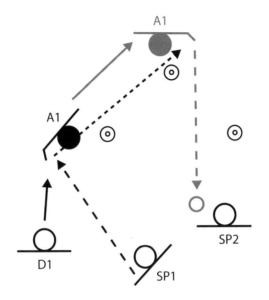

SP2 in this example of playing the ball beyond the oncoming defender becomes the target for the forward pass from A1. Player A1 takes a depth touch and plays the forward pass to player SP2. Player A1 keeps his physical shape, facing the direction of the pass to SP2.

The Result

The defender challenging for the ball – Player A1 takes a depth touch to the ball and plays the ball beyond the defensive player D1.

In any mode of practice all players are encouraged to look up and see what is on, what are the problems and what can he do to solve the problems. Where are the defensive players? What does the player want to do with the ball? Pass it? Keep it? All decisions must be made quickly and of course put into action. In terms of playing skills I will therefore want the players to react quickly and to implement their thoughts just as quickly, if not more so.

Shaping Up

Quick decisions are then changed into physical action. Being able to make the body move in response to the decision has to be trained. Changing the shape of the body to accommodate the touch or the pass against defensive challenges is something that all players should work on. Sometimes players are tired in the game and they just fail to shape up. If that's the case the game moves on but its quality diminishes. Players lose concentration and take touches to the ball with just any part of the boot. The physical shape goes and the passes are no longer accurate. What is interesting though is that once the players lose their discipline they will have to work harder, because when the attention to body shape breaks down players will have to improvise on their touches and pass options even more and in that mode they will work harder because improvisation requires more touches on the ball, not less. In other words, once the players lose their discipline they are unlikely to promote their chances of having a positive effect on the game (depending, of course, on the quality of the opposition). The development of the player should therefore allow him to respond correctly to the problems set before him. In this next example I will use a format that will enable the player to work on changing the shape of his body quickly in response to what is required.

There are a number of seriously important technical and psychological aspects of the game that this format deals with from a practice mode point of view; For Example

1 - The players work on 'Shaping Up' to the touch options

2 – The players work on looking up to see the target/pass direction/player

3 – The players work on getting behind the ball – comfortable position

4 – The players work on two touch options - (a) - The off the line touch to the square on body position and (b) The depth touch option.

5 – The players work on timing their pass – Not too early/to feet

6 - The players work on taking the touch with the correct foot.

7 – The players work on moving to re-position (this habit does away with 'ball watching', admiring the pass rather than making sure that the player is available and therefore open to other play solutions) and of course their fitness - etc

The Practice Format

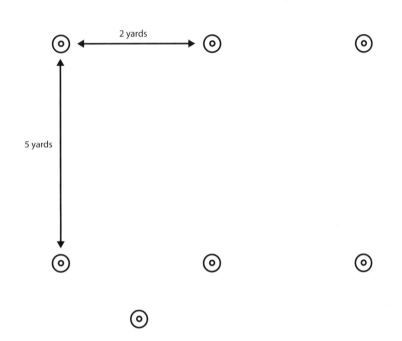

The above format example for practicing shaping up is a combination of the square-on 'two cone' placement and the 'three cone placement'. The off the line touch (two cones) and the Depth touch (three cones) are joined together to enable the players to work on the principles 1 to 7 and on changing their physical shape to accommodate the touch and pass options.

Shape up - The Mirror Effect

In Mode 1

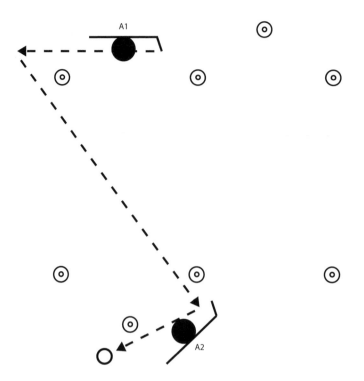

Player's Starting Position

Lets break the movements down so that you can understand exactly how this format works. Player A1 has the ball - From a square on body position A1 moves the ball off the line with the inside instep of his left foot, taking the touch to the ball square on. Once the ball is past the second cone he plays the diagonal pass to player A2 –

As A2 receives the ball, A1 quickly moves across and gets his body shape quarter turned ready and in position, awaiting the return pass from A2.

In Mode 2

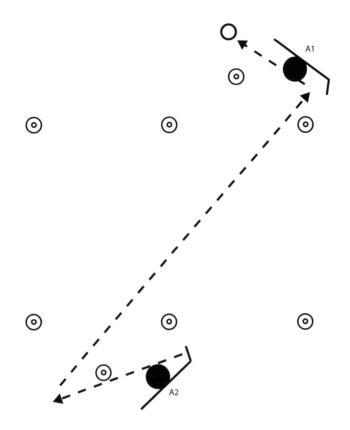

Note – All touch options are about 1.5 yds in length – Therefore the cone placements set on the ground consider that length of touch and are placed accordingly. As for the length of pass, it should be not too long from a practice point of view. As far as the pass itself is concerned we will work on that skill in a separate training session.

In Mode 3

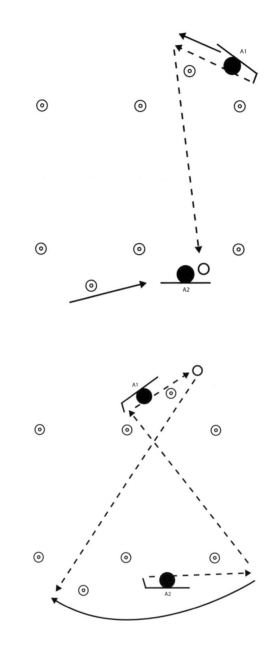

In Mode 4

Player A1 will take a touch to the ball, moving the ball with depth to the back of the cone placement and from there will continue the working sequence by playing the ball across to the now waiting player A2. Player A2 is now in a square on body position. Continue;

48

Shaping Up

The inside instep touch across the body called the 'Off the Line Touch', has a sister touch called 'The extended foot position touch', or simply Extended Touch. This touch is also taken up by the inside instep of the foot. Whether it's the right foot inside instep or the left foot inside instep depends on two playing problems:

1 – Where are the free areas of play – Free of any opponent when the player receives the ball.

2 – Does the player have the time and the space to take the extended touch to the direction of his choice?

The Practice Format - The Practice format couldn't be any simpler to organize.

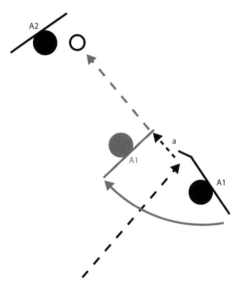

In (a) – Player A1, quarter turned, takes the inside instep of the right foot and touches the ball on to a controlled short touch. The foot extends on the touch to the direction of the touch. The angle of the touch on the ball could vary somewhat. The touch on the ball can set the ball up automatically for the same foot to pass the ball on to player A2 or the angle of the touch can be changed to accommodate the left foot/right foot pass. The same principles apply to both the right or left foot touch options -

A Game Format

The Extended touch option can be applied anywhere on the pitch. The quarter to half turned body position is useful in terms of seeing a larger area of play – The attacking player in the next mode doesn't turn his back to the direction of play. The extended touch option is very good for setting up the action of moving the ball against the defender's position. The touch can be taken and effect a direct 'One on One' playing scenario in an instance where the defender has little or no time to react.

In Mode 1

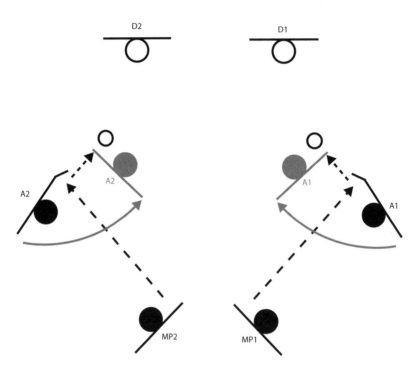

A Game Practice Plan

It is easy to create a game plan when you have a touch option that can begin creative attacking moves. MP1 and MP2 play the ball to, respectively, A2's left foot and A1's right. A1 and A2 attack defenders D1 and D2. Build up the numbers of players in each team from this starting point as follows: MP1 plays the ball to A1, then supports the pass and creates a 2 v 1. Next add MP2 to the mix. Now the defensive player D2 can come in and support his defensive partner D2. At the moment the numbers favor the attacking team, bring in more defenders etc. Play off the touch.

In Mode 2

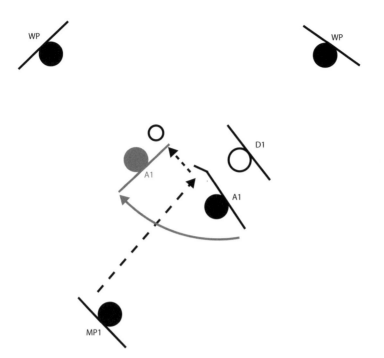

In the above example A1 has applied the extended touch (right foot inside instep), turning on the right shoulder against D1 and moving the ball past him. Player A1 has help to keep the ball from the wide player on his left and the wide player on his right. Again it is possible to build up play from this simple starting point.

The physical shape of the player and appropriate touch options that are applied off the quarter body turn position or square on can make a difference to the success of the player. The position of the body sets the player up for his next play options, making it easier for him to move against defenders or to protect the ball against any opponent trying to win the ball.

Chapter 6 – The Pass Options

Shaping the body up to take up the ball or to make a pass is vital to the quality of the touch and also to the quality of the pass itself. Thus far the players worked on the skill of taking a touch to the ball with the inside instep and playing the pass with the inside instep. But the game of soccer is not just about playing the short pass option. There are also important moments in the game when a longer pass has to be made. For this longer pass, a different foot position is needed, a foot position that will allow the player to apply more power to the pass while maintaining as much control as possible. For this, the best technique is to strike the ball with the top of the foot or laces part of the boot. The physical shape of the body is also different for striking the ball long. While the inside instep pass for short distances is made from a square-on body position, the longer laces of the boot pass is best taken from a sideways-on position. For strong hits on the ball with the laces part of the boot the striking foot comes almost from behind the player's body to the front.

Square On for Short Passes

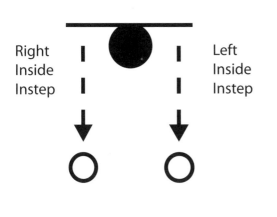

Square on body position = Inside instep Right Foot – Forward Pass
Square on body position = Inside instep Left Foot – Forward Pass

The Long Pass options, on the other hand, are played from a different body shape. The strike of the long ball is performed with the player's body more sideways on.

Example

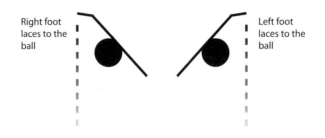

Right foot laces to the ball

Left foot laces to the ball

The following examples of the working formats show a typical training session that concentrates on the practice of passing the ball accurately (within soccer situations) both short and long.

The Introduction Format – The Warm Up

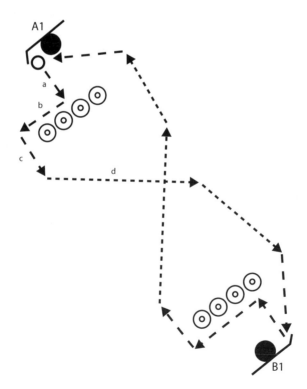

The above format is a good way to bring the player into the correct frame of mind. The pass, for example, is often accompanied by physical effort.

Player A1 takes the ball up from a pass made by B1 and moves the ball with a right foot forward touch towards the cone placement (a). On the second touch A1 moves the ball off the line with his left foot (b). Moving on, A1 takes another forward touch with the right foot (c). At that point he moves the ball with the right foot across to the other side of the format, leaving the cone placements behind him (d).

Note - Moving the ball past the cone placements and cutting across as shown by position (d) in the sequence is intended to simulate the reality of taking on a defender and moving past the defender with the ball and then cutting across the defender's path to leave the defender behind and out of the game. Player A1 will now run to the other side of the format where he will simply pass the ball on to the next player. At the end of the working sequence, the pass from A1 to B1 is performed with the left foot.

Once B1 receives the ball from A1, B1 will try to perform the skills described to the same pattern of physical movements. However, in the interest of equal right and left foot development, he will first move the ball off the line with his right foot whereas player A1 started the working sequence by first moving the ball forward then moving the ball off the line with his left foot.

Moving on – The pass and the body shape to make the pass obviously vary a great deal depending on the playing situation. Technically speaking a pass can be made with almost any part of the body and in the most contorted body shapes you can imagine. There are volleys, half volleys, driven passes, lobbed passes, chipped passes; you name it. We can't simulate every possibility, that's for sure.

What we can do though is to bring in practice formats that will enable the player to develop what can be described as the bread and butter skills of passing. In other words 'The Basics' of passing the ball, with which any player can play a decent game of soccer.

Good Habits

Right foot inside instep – Left foot inside instep;

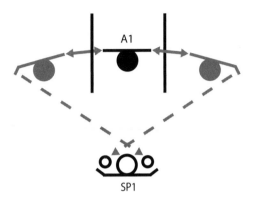

Player A1 moves his body to the ball from behind the format – SP1 plays the ball to the side of the format. Both players concentrate on playing the ball to a specific foot.

In Practice Mode - Player A1 straddles his feet and moves his body to the side of one of the two sticks (right and or left) - to get to the ball. Just a couple of side straddles with his legs to move his body into position behind the ball, to the outside (right and left) of the planted sticks. The pass is made in an alternative manner to the right and left of the sticks. Player A1 responds to the timing of the pass by SP1 who plays the pass alternatively to the right and left foot of player A1. On each return pass A1 moves back between the two sticks - planted. Player A1 passes the ball back to SP1 on each service of the ball – SP1 touch controls the ball and plays it on the second touch.

Hence – A1 - L = left foot pass to the left foot of SP1
A1 – R = Right foot pass to the right foot of SP1

Players take turns- duration of practice 10 min.

The above format is all about getting the players to think about moving physically to get behind the ball and to get into the playing habit of looking up and seeing the value of the pass to the inside (right foot – right foot) (left foot – left foot) of the receiving player. The above format deals with the principles involved in terms of where to play the ball to be most effective.

In Practical Terms

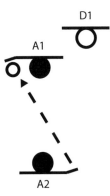

Player A1 – With his back to the attacking line – The habit of moving to the ball physically is also a good habit to have in your locker. Player A1 moves away from the defender and points to his right foot. Player A2 plays the ball with the inside instep of the right foot to the right foot of player A1 – The pass is played to the right foot because player A1 can get to the ball before D1.

The Pass & Move Format
Good Playing Habits

At this next level, the theme of the practice is still to get behind the ball. However, here we will also look at things like calling for the ball at the right time. In this example the call 'Yes!' comes once the player is through each gate. 'Yes!' is a shout to SP1 that means "Pass me the ball!". In this format the player works on moving forward to the ball, making sure that the pass back to SP1/SP2 is then played with the foot following through on contact with the ball. When moving forward, the pass back to the service player is played with the inside instep of either foot. SP1 at each side of the format will pass/play the ball: on the left of the format to the player's call and left foot, on the right of the format to the player's right foot.

The working sequence – Pass and move – The habit of passing the ball and moving to re-position for a possible return pass or to support other players is part of the work. After the pass back is performed the player veers away and turns to move quickly to the next gate on the other side. Why the gates? In this format the gates (sticks positioned in that configuration) on either side are there for a purpose. They are there to make sure the player is upright and moving forward when the ball comes to him from SP1/SP2 – The inside instep pass back is best played from a forward moving body position and from an upright body position. The gates on either side of the format are there to make sure that this is the case. It is always best if the player receiving the ball helps the passer of the ball. Coming to the ball is a good way of making sure that the pass is successful;

For Example

A)   ## B)

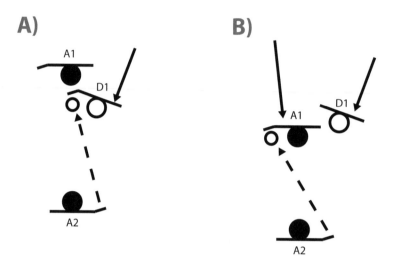

In Mode (a) – Player A1 Failed To Move To The Ball – Sometimes a good pass is made to look bad not because A2 didn't play a decent pass but simply because player A1 failed to come to the ball.

In Mode (b) – Player A1 has supported the pass and the pass is successful.

In Playing Terms

There is an important playing moment in the attacking phase of the game where all of the above references come into play. Keeping possession of the ball while making progress towards the opponent's goal and therefore creating the playing solutions that achieve certain objectives like creating forward moving options that end with a goal for example, requires the application of different skills. The physical shape of the player needs to be utilized to good effect. For example;

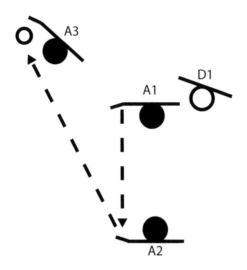

In this example of the effects of the work carried out the players have worked out a typical playing scenario.
Player A1 (diagram (b) on the previous page) comes short and plays the ball back to player A2. Here, A2 then passes the ball on to A3, thus making forward progress. All such habits and therefore playing skills help the players to keep the ball and make forward moving progress towards their target which is of course to score goals and win games.

The Shape Of The Format

All formats have one thing in common with the player. The player and his starting position are part and parcel of the way the format works.

In Practice Mode

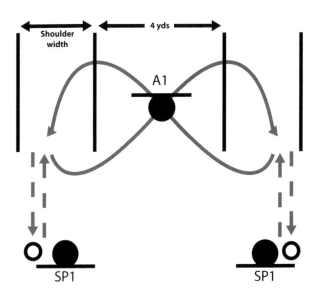

SP1 /SP2 pass the ball to player A1.
A1 passes the ball back to SP1/SP2 and moves to the next pass back option.

The Practice Format - Player A1 runs in a figure 8 pattern, receiving the pass/ball from SP1/SP2 in turn and making a pass back: Through the left gate as we look - Right foot pass back to SP1 – On the right as we look player A1 plays the left foot pass back to player SP2. When playing the pass or playing the ball back – players play the ball to the correct foot.

L = A1 left foot pass back to SP2's Right foot
R = A1 right foot pass back to SP1's Left foot

Player A1 moves in a figure eight pattern to the back of the two sticks on either side of the format and from the back through to the front through and between the two sticks. A1 will call for the ball in order to get the ball. SP1/2 times his pass to the call made. Player A1 plays the ball back to SP1/2 – This is a pass and move configuration.

In this format we also work on and develop the players' two footedness. That goes without saying now. The player always applies the right and left foot pass capability. Such formats go hand in hand with the single line of cones that deals with the development of the strength of the player on the weak side of the body. This is because we are always working to make sure that the practice format enables the player to work on both the right and left side of the body. Thus we ensure the development of the players' strength on both sides of the body and therefore their ability to play the ball with the left foot and the right foot to any playing solution of choice – The neutral formats (no bias in terms of which foot the player works with) ensure the correct physical development in all manner of ways from the technical to the physical requirements of the players.

The Diagonal Pass Option
Practice Format

The following format works to the same principles as previously explained. There are minor differences. Since the players have dealt with the practice of passing the ball forward with the inside instep we will now want the players to practice passing the ball with the laces of the right or left boot diagonally.

The Diagonal Pass

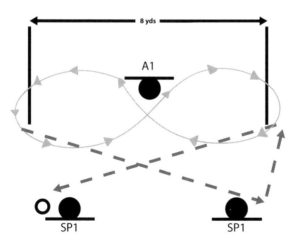

Laces To The Ball

The pass with the right and left foot (laces to the ball) will also be practiced with a figure eight run – The ball by SP1/2 is played as A1 comes out of the turn.

SP1/2 plays the ball to the side, as shown. The diagonal arrows show the pass back to the diagonal angle by player A1.

Return Pass - Player A1 = L – Left foot laces diagonal pass to player SP1 - Player A1 = R – Right foot laces diagonal pass to player SP2

The diagonal pass is extremely useful in the final third of the pitch, especially if the defense is holding their line high up the pitch.

For Example

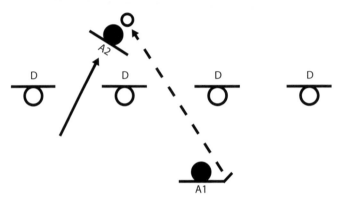

A2 times his run to perfection, breaks through the defense and takes advantage of the diagonal pass played by player A1.

The Long & Short Pass Combination

One of the easiest working formats that enables the player to work on the short and long pass options (once the players are familiar with the pass to a specific foot) is a two stick configuration placed at an angle that enables the ball to be played to a one two pass option. In this format the players work on;

1 –Passing the ball on first contact on the ball.

Note – I said 'first contact on the ball' – I didn't say 'first touch'. This is a controversial opinion. I base my opinion, however, on the fact that I think there is a difference between playing the ball on first contact and taking a touch to the ball. A touch to the ball is a touch to the ball – A pass is a pass. The two to my way of thinking are not one and the same thing technically speaking. I will try to highlight what is involved when I present the work on 'The Actual First Touch Options' later on.

Back to Business -

2 – Play the ball to a specific foot - Back to basics and the understanding of playing the ball to the front of the runner.

3 – Set The Ball Up - Play the ball in such a way that it is played not only to the correct foot but to the angle that enables the next player to pass the long ball to the third man in the working format. Thus helping the players to practice the short and long pass play combination.

In Practice Mode

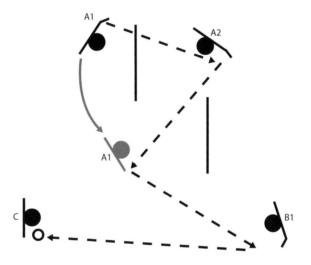

Players A1 and B1 work the ball towards the bottom of the page - A1 and B1 play the pass on first contact to the ball past the sticks that in effect simulate the position of opponents (defenders are not in play). The players can work the ball back and forwards around the sticks two times before working the final pass option that sets B1 up for the long pass option. The final pass from A1 to B1 is not played to feet but to the side and ahead of him. B1 passes the ball long with the laces of the left boot to player C.

A Game Format

The players are aware of the passing possibilities: Playing the ball to feet, which foot, whether to make the pass short or long etc. Organizing a game of soccer that has a specific starting point is now easy enough. The players have the basics in hand. The pass can be played without the ball ever touching the ground, which of course goes without saying. We wont be doing that here but we have enough basics in terms of the pass and touch options here to put on a training session that deals with the pass to space, feet, short and long and that's enough for a really good training session.

PASS THE BALL TO THE FRONT MEN ST1 – ST2

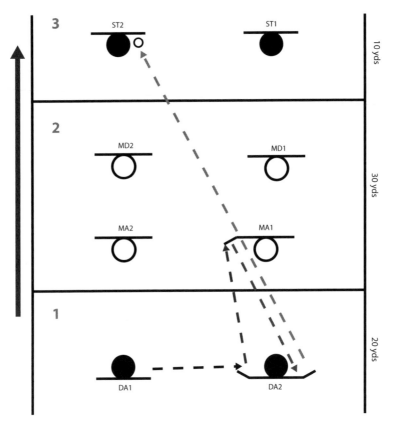

The Pass Zone

Players in zone 1 work the ball to the midfield players A1 and A2 inside zone 2. In that zone the midfield players have a license to keep the ball, take the opposing midfield player on if they wish, pass to an attacker in zone 3 or play back to a defender in zone 1 who would restart the play with either a ball back to the midfield or a long pass to the strikers up front in zone 3. Once the ball is with ST1 or ST2, play continues in the opposite direction.

Players sometimes do work in channels because keeping the system of play (team shape) is important to keeping possession.

Chapter 7 - One On One 'Playing Skills'

By now you may have already guessed that the two footedness of the player is not something that we condition but something that we simply work on automatically by virtue of the way we work. All the working formats in this book are designed in a way that simply enables the player to work on both the right and the left foot capability. The skills go hand in hand with the physical and technical development through the natural endeavours that develop the physical capability and therefore the good playing habits that result from this kind of work.

The Enforcer

Sounds a bit ominous. The title is appropriate for my next point of view. The first objective in the quest to develop the 'One on One' ability, taking on defensive positions or indeed simply protecting the loss of the ball on an individual basis is to develop the player's ability to use the ball effectively with the inside instep of the foot and or the underside of the foot and or even the outside of the foot when protecting the ball or if you like dribbling with the ball against the opposition. The skills in question either protect the ball from being lost to the opposition or enable the player in possession of the ball to take on one or more defenders.

Note – The skills we will look at are for the purpose of the team game, they are not for the purpose of looking good on the ball. The game of soccer is a team game and the skills are there to help the team win games.

Back To Business

The enforcer happens to be the 'Single Line Of Cones' lateral movement format. This format is used often to make sure that players are on the right track, so to speak. Going back to this format keeps the players on top of their skills because the basis for all individual skills of soccer consist of the work within the single line of cones. The additional skill of 'moving the ball off the line' is added on at the appropriate moment. It is a format that always helps them to keep in touch with the basics of One on One Skills and other touches on the ball that include the 'First Touch Options' – Why? Because the lateral development format keeps the player physically in tune with the lateral movements that actually prevail in the game of soccer, perhaps even more than any forward moving skill, other than running of course.

The Lateral Format

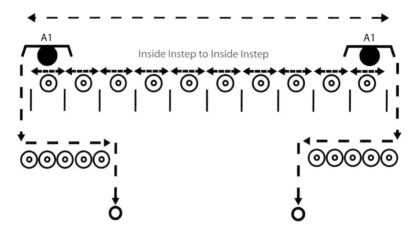

Inside Instep to Inside Instep

Bread & Butter Skills

What is the big deal here then? Loads! Looks a bit messy though, and complicated. Lets tidy it up. In the above format there are physical movements that are seriously valuable to the development of the One on One skills. The inside instep work, playing the ball from gap to gap parallel with the line of cones (lateral development guideline) develops the necessary leg to leg co-ordination that is very important to the ability of the player to work the ball to a combination of touch options.

The inside instep movements of the ball from foot to foot to the end of the line of cones develops a physical effect, one of ball control and the ability to play the ball from one foot (inside instep) to the next. The additional cone placements to the front of the single line of cones begin the player's journey on the ability to take on defenders. The touch options taken begin with the right or left foot to the ball depending on the position of the opponent. The forward touch of the ball is a challenging touch that is linked to a one on one skill that you have already seen, 'Moving the ball off the line', which is also effective when the underside of the foot is used to move the ball to the side of the challenging opponent. The cone placements in front of the line of cones simulate the position of the defensive player (defender not in place) - We will practice the inside instep short movements here and obviously bring the movements worked on to other working shapes that create the 'One on One' playing solutions.

IN PLAYING MODE
For Example

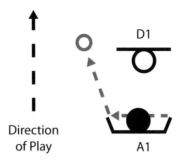

Direction
of Play

D1

A1

A Two Footed Touch Combination

Right inside instep touch moves the ball to the side – Left inside instep moves the ball forward and away from the opponent D1.

In the above playing scenario, D1 would have won the ball if it wasn't for A1's ability to apply the left and right foot combination that moved the ball and the player away from the challenging foot of player D1. This is a simple side to forward touch combination, effective yet simple to apply. Such skills can be called 'One On One' playing skills – The development of such skills requires a working format that is specific to the task.

The Development Of 'One On One' Playing Skills

There are several important technical and physical problems that we have to work on in order to develop the player's ability to play 'One on One' Skills. In the above example player A1 took two touches to the ball, one with the right foot inside instep that moved the ball to the left side of the player and one with the other foot (left foot) that moved the ball past the defensive player D1. In the single line of cones (the lateral development format) players work on the short inside instep touches. All of that effort is in keeping with the aims of the training session, which are:

1 – The development of the player's Two Footedness – This requires the development of the player's physical ability to be equally strong on both the right and left side of the body.

2 – The development of the player's physical ability to apply specific physical movements to the ball, that in effect work the ball to the solutions required when dealing with the challenger 'One On One'.

The 'One On One' Skill Combination Format Examples

Note - The following assumes that all players are proficient at working the ball with the inside instep alternative foot to the ball parallel to and down the line of cones.

The Practical

The inside instep movements do not now obviously go down any line of cones. Here we are going to employ the inside instep movements to a physical working pattern that deals with the reality of facing an opponent. When the player is faced with an opponent he has to take evasive action. Lets go through what is going on in the following format.

First Things First

In some formats we begin the work by allowing the players to work out the movements involved without the ball. The physical movements without the ball are obviously easier to do. The idea is to get the players familiar with the movements, to know what the working pattern means from a skills perspective.

The way the cones have been placed on the ground is not earth shattering stuff, I know. Nonetheless, it's a useful way of introducing the player to the skills required for success in 1v1 confrontations. In this format the players work out the pattern and realize that in effect what they are working on are changes in the direction of their movements, to the left, to the right and so on and experiencing the lateral to forward changes in the direction of the work. Lateral movements on their own don't amount to much, but the cone placements provide a frame of reference that gives the players the feedback they need to understand that what they are working on is the change of angle attitude and therefore the lateral to forward, left to right, right to left changes in direction.

◆ ▬ ▬ ▬ ➡ This represents inside instep movements without the ball (side straddle feet to the gaps).

O

◆ ▬ ▬ ▬ ➡ This represents inside instep movements with the ball.

The 'lateral to forward' changes in directions are worked on with and without the ball for best effect.

68

In Playing Mode

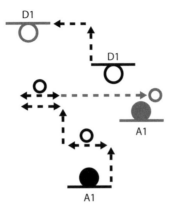

The defensive player reacted to the touches but then the attacking player did a double take and moved the ball to his right. Such changes in direction are essential to keeping the ball.

In Practice Mode
Practice 'Skill Patterns' - Physical Movements – With & Without The Ball.

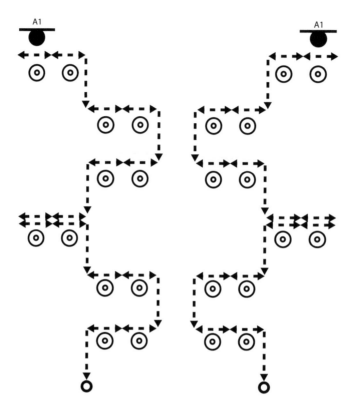

Note – The cone placement pattern is set up to this configuration in order to concentrate more on the development of the physical strength. All extensive working formats are fitness orientated, as you will note. For actual skill orientation, that is to say, the 'One on One' skill patterns, the cone placements are absolutely reduced to the relevant working parts only.

For Example – In Practice Mode

The Skill – Inverted Steps – Its function – Avoiding loss of possession through a challenge for the ball.

In Practice Mode

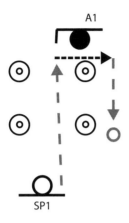

Length of touch - shoulder width
1. Off the Line Touch with right inside instep
2. Forward Touch with left inside instep

In Playing Mode

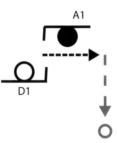

Note – The combination of touches to the ball begins with the foot that matches the challenger. If the challenger uses his right foot then the attacking player, the player in possession of the ball, also needs to move the ball away from the challenger's foot by using the right foot. In this example the right foot (inside instep) moves the ball out of D1's reach. We gave the playing example of this double foot action skill at the beginning of the chapter.

To Organize - The practice format is easy to organize. It is just four cones set to almost a square. To keep the player working, SP1 touches the ball on to the next player (player A1) - The set distance between the cone placements is according to the shoulder width of the player, to the configuration shown. The side to forward touch combination of the right to left foot movement is done in sequence. The feet move quickly; Right foot - left foot - forward touch. Don't forget the working sequence is just as easy the other way; Left foot - right foot - forward touch.

In this next example, the player will double up on that skill in order to deal with two challengers for the ball. This can be performed in to ways;

71

1 - The double application of the 'Inverted Touch' Combination

2 – The 'Inverted Touch' is combined with the 'Off the line touch'
The off the line touch can be played with the underside of the boot or the inside instep. If the ball is played with the underside of the boot this is a faster movement of the foot because the foot sweeps over the ball.

The Double Inverted Steps Format
In Practice Mode

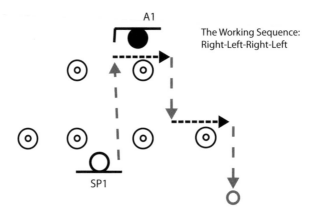

The Working Sequence:
Right-Left-Right-Left

In Playing Mode

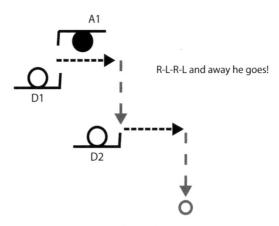

R-L-R-L and away he goes!

Note - I hope you don't think I have been lazy in not giving you the examples on the left foot. The actions of the left side of the player are to the same movement sequence, it is just that the work begins with the left foot and not the right foot. The working sequence with the right foot is; RLRF - The working sequence with the ball by the left foot is; LRLF. It's that simple.

The Double Skill Combination
Inverted Steps & Off the line touch

In the following example of a combined skills option I will use the left foot to start the working sequence. Here though the player has a choice of either playing the inside instep to affect the second part of the movement or applying the underside of the boot to the ball against the second defensive player.

Unlike the above format, this next example is slightly different in that the shape in the second part of the format is changed to accommodate the practice alternative of playing the faster sweep action.
The decision on which touch to use in a real game of soccer depends on the situation. If the second challenger, for example, is very close to the player in possession of the ball he may be forced to use the sweep over the ball to get away.

In Practice Mode

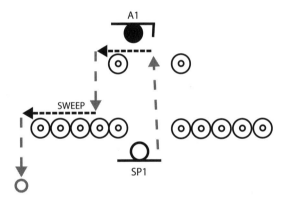

Note - All touches played with the 'Leading foot' are played to a length that makes it easy for the other foot to play the next touch.

Alternatively, the left foot action in the 'SECOND PART' of the movement (moving the ball against the five cone placements) in this format can be played with the inside instep. However, if it is played with the inside instep of the left foot the movement is effectively slower than if it is played with the underside of the boot to sweep over the ball. The sweep over the ball obviously is a faster skill option. When is it played? It depends on how much time the player has against the challengers.

Different Solutions

The above examples dealt with the problems of keeping the ball against a very close opponent who can almost touch the ball. In some ways such situations where the opponent is eager and is putting his foot to the ball can be easier to deal with than facing an opponent that's a lot more clever about the way he defends or tries to win the ball. In this next couple of examples of 'One on One' playing skills we will look at the kind of skills you need in order to deal with a more patient opponent;

In Practice Mode
The Double Bluff

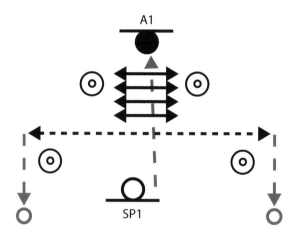

The two feet inside instep in action – The ball is moved from inside instep to inside instep as quickly as the player can, moving the ball and himself through the first set of two cones that make a gap for him to go through. Once through the gap the player then moves the ball off the line to either the left or right of his square on body position. Note that in order to move the ball off the line to the left the player needs to apply the right foot inside instep to the ball and vice versa. Again, just like with the previous skill options, the second part of the movement here can also be played with the underside of the boot sweeping the ball off the line.

In Playing Mode
The First Part Of The Movement

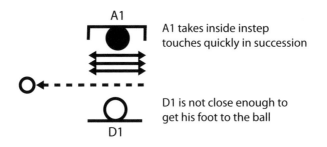

A1 takes inside instep touches quickly in succession

D1 is not close enough to get his foot to the ball

Player A1 takes advantage of the distance between himself and the defensive player and takes touches to the ball that will enable him to either go past the defensive player or to simply make sure that he doesn't lose possession of the ball. A1 can move the ball to any direction, at any time during this touch sequence.

In Playing Mode
The End Product

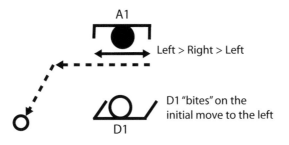

Left > Right > Left

D1 "bites" on the initial move to the left

Disguise

How many touches? In all but one example above, player A1 took four touches to the ball before moving the ball off the line to his right.

In this example it is the inside instep of the left foot that starts off the working sequence. Player A1 applies a quick touch sequence of three touches to the ball (including moving the ball off the line) - All touch options are designed to keep the ball. The touch sequence can vary, from one touch to four or five touches on the ball. - When the left foot touched the ball onto the right foot in the above example, player D1 could easily buy into the idea that player A1 will keep the ball moving in that direction. So! When the player then touched the ball back onto his left foot it certainly confused D1, especially because it was done quickly. The final part of the movement takes place with player A1 moving the ball off the line with the underside of his left boot. Player A1 in the above example actually took four touches to the ball to affect his playing solution. The ball was touched on from the left foot inside instep to the right foot inside instep then back to the inside instep of the left foot, at which point the inside instep of the left foot moved the ball off the line and the move was finished off by applying the final forward touch to the ball to get away from the challenging player D1. What happens after that is the application of whatever player A1 wants to do with the ball.

How many touches to create an effective action? Obviously this all depends on the situation. In any case the player can get away with the ball to any direction at any time, to as little as a one touch and one off the line move option.

For Example

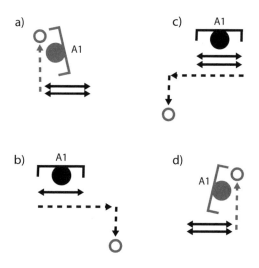

In (a) – Inside instep x 2 drag back and turn to the right.
In (b) – Inside instep x 1 and move the ball off the line
In (c) – Inside instep x 2 and move the ball to the right
In (d) – Inside instep x 2 drag the ball and turn to the left.

The player can go forward of the defender and he can also just as easily turn away with the ball.

Strength Development – Fast Feet

The final moments of getting away from the defensive player requires strength and therefore precise and fast footwork. Here is a simple way of practicing the fast feet get away; -

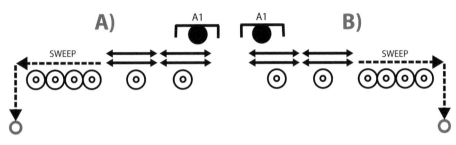

(a) – The left foot inside instep starts the working sequence; Inside instep – Inside instep – Sweep – Forward touch.

(b) – The right foot inside instep starts the working sequence; Inside instep – Inside instep – Sweep – Forward touch.

Note – Formats like the above example are good starting points for the practice of moving in support of the touch and pass. I will do some examples of that later.

A Give Way Touch Option

Sometimes, not very often I hasten to say, the defensive player may well be forced to give ground. This happens when the defensive player is the only player that can stall the attacking play. In such a situation the defensive player may well hold up play by employing what is an old fashioned expression 'jockeying the attacking player' – holding up play is probably a better expression for this next example.

In Playing Mode
D1 BACKS OFF

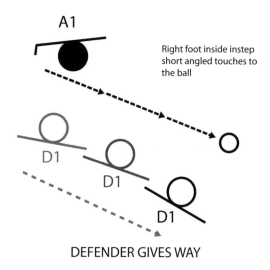

A1

Right foot inside instep
short angled touches to
the ball

D1

D1

D1

DEFENDER GIVES WAY

Basically – The defensive player doesn't go for/to the ball, all he is doing is trying to slow the game down. It is not a good idea but that's what can happen on the rare occasions when the defense is caught short.

Still In Playing Mode
The Problem For The Defensive Player D1

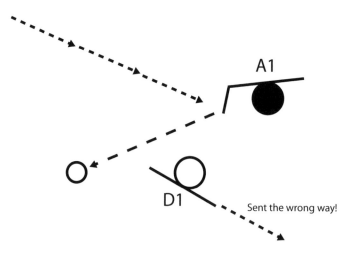

A1

D1

Sent the wrong way!

At some point in the touch sequence the attacking player can lose the defender by taking the ball on the outside of the boot and changing the shape of the body to move the ball diagonally to the right of player A1. In effect the touches are taken with the inside instep of the right/left foot. In the above example, it happens to be the inside instep of the right foot. At the appropriate moment (when the attacking player A1 thinks D1 is out of shape and out of balance) player A1 takes the outside of the boot to the ball, changes directions and hopefully loses his marker D1.

In Practice Mode

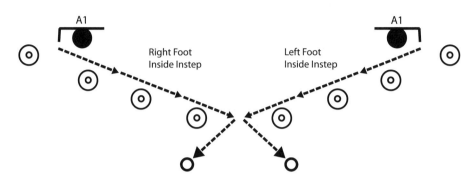

Take the inside instep touch to the ball to each gap in the cone placements. At the end of the angled cone line, escape by playing the ball with the outside of the boot. Right foot, right foot, right foot (ORF - Escape outside of the right boot) – Left foot, left foot, left foot (OLF Escape outside of the left boot/foot).

Playing The Skills Off The First Touch

There are times in the game where it is natural to have to move the ball against a defensive player that is right in your face when you least expect it. To effectively deal with that situation, the player needs a way of practicing for such moments. I find that the best way is to take the player into a working format that enables him to take a touch to the ball and then apply an 'off the first touch option'. In normal play circumstances I wouldn't expect any player to take a touch to the ball that would put him into trouble. The point of this next format is to try to simulate a common event in the game of soccer, namely, taking a touch to the ball and having to deal with a challenger that's come from nowhere.

Playing Off The First Touch

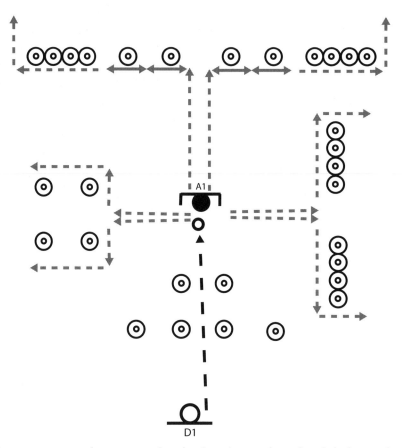

I don't expect you to know exactly what's going on here but I do hope that you recognize the working shapes surrounding player A1 in this format. You need to know the first touch options if you want to practice keeping the ball to the above considerations. My next chapter will deal with the development of a number of first touch options to the ball that in effect underpin all working solutions and therefore all practice formats.

Chapter 8 – The First Touch & The Playing Problems

The inside instep position is exceptionally effective in helping the player to control the ball in a meaningful way. In the following chapter we will work on and describe first touch options that are effective and meaningful to the game of soccer. One of the most important reasons for the existence of the following first touch options is that in their performance we have the weapons to deal with any number of playing problems. I don't believe that you can play effective soccer without the following first touch options. In addition, I don't believe that you can work on any number of soccer related formats if your starting positions are obscured by what I call improvisational start ups. This is because I believe that if you have a meaningful start up (with a specific skill application) to any training sequence then that makes the right impression on the players and therefore they will remember the skills in use more readily. In the previous format, where we want to empower the player to play off the first touch, we know that none of that would be possible if the player didn't know any first touch options. That's the reason I did not describe the workings of the format. However, once you have read this chapter you will be able to work out what the format is all about.

The First Objective

All good ball control skills have a common feature. The common feature throughout the sporting world is called the follow through. In soccer terms, good ball control means that the touch on the ball is performed well if the foot on contact with the ball moves in the direction of the touch to the ball. That's called 'The Follow Through'.

We talked about shaping up because that too is also important. When it comes to the development of the player's skills, all movements within formats go hand in hand with the requirements of the player's physical development. It is important that the player is strong, but in the right way for soccer. This to me is an important issue. The player's strength to play soccer should come mainly from what he does on the practice ground and during the game. The actual working formats should cover at least eighty percent of the player's physical requirements. The other twenty per cent should come from other activities. There are all kinds of endeavours on the training ground that can be effective in developing the player's natural strength, like running for example. Working out in formats like the ones I'm describing and many others that I haven't described yet ensures that there is no shortage of ideas that will develop the player's natural strength and therefore his playing capability by the time he is in his early twenties. In this next example there are important physical objectives that we will meet. Strength development through physical action is one of them. The development of the physical side of the player on both the right and left of his physical being is another. Looking up off the side touch (the lateral angle touch) - The development of the strength in the inner groin. The ability to move the ball to the lateral angle and to drop the shoulder in action, to move the body one way and to go with the ball to the opposite direction is another. To follow through on the touch is of course the main theme of the practice format.

The Follow Through Development Format

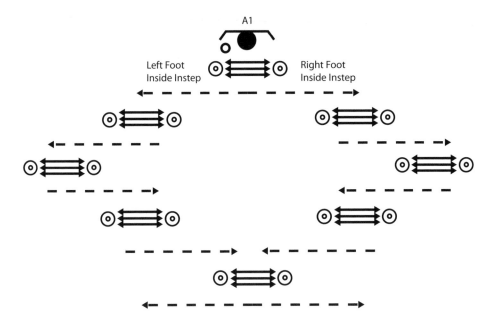

Follow Through Format

The above follow through format deals with a number of development issues. The development of the player's strength through the application of the lateral movements will become obviously more relevant to you when we look at the first touch development and the movements involved within the performance of most first touch options. Staying square on becomes more understandable when you apply the physical solutions to many playing problems. The above format is one of the most effective development tools for the ability to follow through on the touch of the ball. If you go back to the skill of moving the ball off the line you will note that the touch played with the inside instep of the right or the left foot to the ball is similar to the design of the above format. The movements in the above format are in practical terms exactly the same, the only difference being the amount of movements both in terms of the physical inside instep short actions on the ball and the 'off the line movements'. This

82

format is foundational to the skill of moving the ball off the line. The format and the skill in use is not a coincidence, all formats are directly related. In fact all the formats are directly linked to the principles of two footedness. The follow through is an essential prerequisite to quality first touch options on the ball.

Lateral Strength Development

The development of the player's inner groin strength and the development of his equal strength on both the right and left side of the body is achieved through the physical movements set in formats like the above example. In this example the short arrow indicators represent the touches taken to the ball with the inside instep of either foot and the longer arrow points to the physical movements that move the ball off the line to the lateral angle.

The short inside instep to the ball movements are joined up to the longer off the line length of touch. The players should be encouraged to move the foot across the body when moving the ball off the line to the left or right of the working format.

Note - The off the line touch played with the inside instep of the foot or the outside of the boot to the lateral angle is shown by the longer arrow.

Note - In examining the above format you will notice that the concentration of the work does not include the forward touch. The main reason for that is that we want the players to concentrate all their efforts on their lateral development, especially in the areas of the follow through and the touch that makes sure the ball is played to the lateral angle.

The first of the first touch options we will look at is coincidently the touch of 'Moving the ball off the line'. If the player can master this touch, he will be able to play a more effective game of soccer. Looking up off a meaningful touch helps the player to create more playing options because he can see more of the playing field. Players who improvise often have their head down and see less, not more, of their playing solutions. In learning to take a meaningful first touch, players take the first steps to open up their playing domain.

The First Touch Development
'Moving the ball off the line'

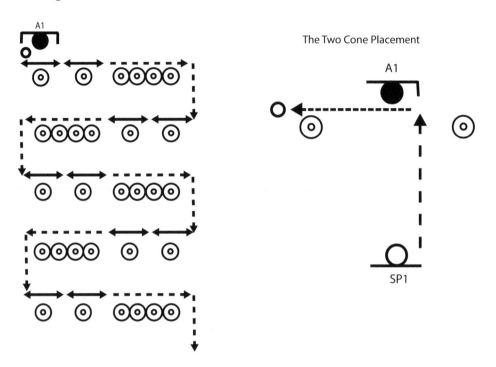

The Two Cone Placement

Reduced For Effect
What we have here is a format that takes in the lateral development efforts of the previous more physically demanding work and reduces the actions to a defined level for the purpose of targeting the 'Moving the ball off the line' touch.

Note – From a playing point of view - The length of touch when performing the 'Moving the ball off the line' skill is approx 1.5 yds. So, the two cone placements are about 3. 5 yds apart. The width of the cone placement depends on the age of the players. If you are dealing with very young players, obviously the length of touch on the ball would not be that long and so the position of the cone placements on the ground would have to deal with that reality. The cone placements are important however, as you will hopefully note when I explain their relevance to the scheme of things.

Back To Business - Obviously the actions of moving the ball off the line are specific to a certain playing scenario and we now need to define this more clearly. Format A1 is designed to work very specifically on the 'Moving the ball off the line' touch.

84

In Practice Mode

The working sequence is as follows:
✓   The right foot inside instep moves the ball short and the left foot inside instep stops the ball momentarily
✓   Repeat this sequence in the other direction – The right foot inside instep moves the ball short and the left foot inside instep stops the ball momentarily
✓   Next – Moving the ball with the inside instep of the right foot, move the ball to the off the line touch and then take the forward touch to the ball with the inside instep of the left foot.
✓   That sequence of touches on the ball with the inside instep of both feet completes the first part of the working sequence.
✓   The forward touch moves the player to the next section in the format where he will begin the working sequence again but this time with the inside instep of the left foot.
✓   Inside instep - Inside instep - Touch on – Forward touch – Inside instep - Inside instep - Touch on - Forward touch and so on rhythmically and without pausing, the player works the ball down the format to a given sequence (position of the cone placements in the format) of touches on the ball.

The Development Of The First Touch; -
'Moving The Ball Off The Line'

We have looked at the physical movements involved in 'Moving the ball off the line'. This touch can be played when the player already has possession of the ball and we have in fact seen that previously, on many occasions. We have also talked about the two ways that this touch can be played;

1 - With the inside instep
2 - With the underside of the boot that swipes over the top of the ball.

Forget the underside of the boot when you are taking the ball off a pass and playing the ball off the line as a first touch option. The safest way of taking up the ball from a pass, if the ball is coming on the ground that is, is with the inside instep. When the pass in made to the feet, the touch has certain technical requirements. There are differences in moving the ball off the line as a first touch option. This touch can be played when the ball comes from a pass but there are technical skills in taking up the pass that need to be developed for the first touch to be effective.

In Terms Of Decision Making

Which touch to the ball? What is the best first touch option? A good player will always have several things in mind when he is about to receive the ball. Training sessions where the players are not allowed to develop the skills of assessing what is on worry me. When I was watching a game of five a sides played by young children I thought, "How could any young player develop this side of the game in a game that doesn't allow him to look up and see anything or that doesn't allow him to take a decent touch to the ball?". Making decisions in such an environment is difficult enough, but implementing them when you haven't got the skills and you are effectively one footed is impossible. What the players need are working formats that empower them to make decisions and have the right skill to make them work. To make the right decisions and to have the ability to implement such decisions, that's what needs to happen. Before any player receives the ball he needs to assess his own position on the field of play. He then also needs to know the following;

1 - The position of his own players.
2 - The position of the opposing players
3 - The weak points in the opponent's line up
4 - What touch option to apply in order to affect play;-

Taking away from the players the ability to choose their playing options is wrong. I would have to ask questions as to why anyone would think otherwise. In this natural world of the one handed (right handed) mentality, conditioning players on how to play soccer has become the fashionable thing to do. The favorite way of playing has become 'Keeping the ball at the feet'. This is the first thought in most players' heads now. Why is that? The first thought in any good player's head should be, "How can I create the most effective playing solution?". This requires a different approach to the one footedness reality that has emerged over the last twenty or so years as a means of coaching and playing soccer, which has in practical terms led to some of the negative play solutions that have been part of the game for years. The effective development of any soccer player should make the player realize and appreciate a whole range of soccer playing skills. Here is a simple fact of life:

If it is the case that a player cannot play the ball equally well with the left foot or the right foot then he is only able to take advantage of 50% of the playing skills on offer.

100 % - The development of the two footedness of the player and the development of a decent touch to the ball makes all the difference to the player's opportunity to play a better game of soccer. This is not down to opinion, it is fact. These skills are not optional, they are the bread and butter

skills with which to play effective soccer. What is so special about the right and left foot working sequence in the above example, then? In such formats the player works on and develops the correct physical attributes for playing soccer.

In Practice Mode

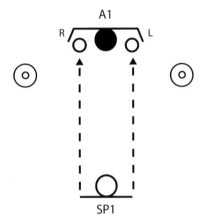

The player's central role, and therefore his physical position within the format, creates certain technical guidelines that he will work with in his quest to develop a good first touch to the ball. What are the key issues here?

Taking The Touch

1 – SP1 – The service player will play the ball to either the left or the right foot.

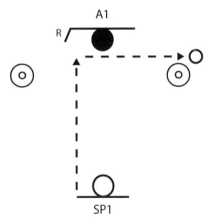

When the ball arrives on the right foot inside instep of player A1, he will look down on the ball and put his right foot out towards the ball. His left foot then moves slightly back and keeping himself square on he touches the ball on across his body to his left. He keeps his eyes forward as the ball moves to the side. At this point the player either passes the ball on or keeps the ball.

1 – MOVEMENT OPTIONS

1 - The player takes the ball up with the inside instep of the right foot, making sure that the foot follows the ball across the body. He simply brings himself with the ball across the format to the position shown. From then on the player has a choice of actions that he could take.

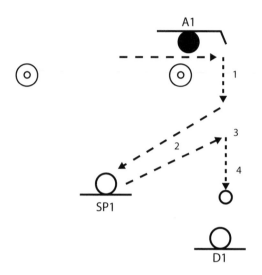

1 – A1 takes a forward touch to the ball with the inside instep of the left foot getting to the ball

2 – A1 plays a pass to SP1 and SP1 returns the pass

3 – A1 takes up the ball with the inside instep of the left foot

4 – At this point A1 can take D1 on and apply one of the 'One on One' skill options.

ALTERNATIVELY

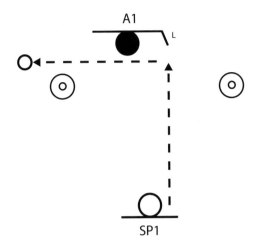

In Practice Mode

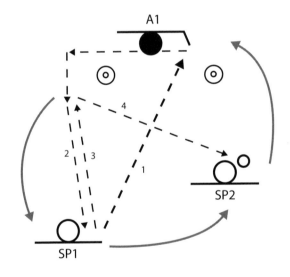

The starting point – SP1 plays the ball to the left foot inside instep of player A1. A1 changes the angle of the ball and takes a touch with the inside instep of his left foot, moving the ball to his right, keeping square on and making sure he follows through on the touch. He then takes a forward touch with his right inside instep, plays a long ball to player SP1 and supports the pass. SP1 passes back to A1 on first contact and A1 passes to SP2, also on first contact. SP2 then passes to A1 and the three players exchange positions; A1 to SP1, SP1 to SP2 and SP2 to A1 to start again.

The above practice cannot be done effectively without thinking about what the players are doing. When player A1 takes the forward touch to the ball he knows that his line of support for his pass to player SP1 will have to be to his right and to the left of player SP2. Player A1, knowing that he will play the ball on to SP2, must make the long pass to SP1's right side. Why? Because he knows that he will have to shape up to receive the ball on his left foot from SP1 to have the best chance of playing an accurate first contact pass to SP2.

The coaching of players should go along the lines that I have described because the two footedness of the player is the better way forward.

The players should know that in movement terms fast interchange positional play requires the pass to be made on first contact. That's why everything is done with such things in mind. For example, the quality of the touch (weight of touch for control), the quality of the pass (accuracy – strength), passing to the appropriate foot, the run, to which angle, and so on. All of that is important if we want to produce a higher standard of play.

The Forward Touch

What is a forward touch to the ball? The forward touch on the ball is played with the inside instep of the foot. Some players can take a forward touch to the ball with the outside of the boot but that means twisting the foot around. The forward touch on the ball is usually played with the inside instep of the foot and obviously can be played when the player is already in possession of the ball or when the ball is received as a first touch option. There are lots of uses for the forward touch. We have seen the forward touch used in previous examples. The forward touch is a touch that in effect takes the ball forward of the player in away that enables him to implement important playing solutions.

In Playing Mode
The Right Foot Forward Touch & Pass Options

For Example

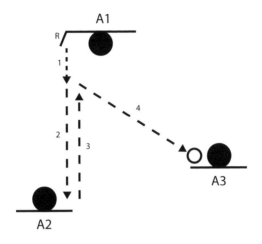

Taking the right foot touch – The pass – forward & diagonal
In the above example, the inside instep takes the ball forward of player A1 and into a position that enables him to play first a forward return pass to A2, then a diagonal pass to A3.

1 – Right Foot Forward Touch
2 – The Forward Pass to A2
3 – The return pass by player A2
4 – The diagonal pass off the forward touch to A3

Note – Off the forward touch, the diagonal pass is easier to make than the forward touch because the forward touch requires an unnatural outward turn of the foot.

The Left Foot Forward Touch & Pass Options

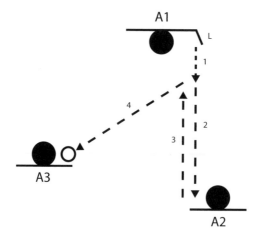

First touch options are essential to the solutions that the player needs to implement. However, a lack of two - footedness in players is a problem from a decision making point of view. For example, if an out and out one footed player sees what he needs to do but the playing options are to his wrong side, he will need to take several touches to the ball to achieve his objective. This would of course cost both time and physical effort, not only for the player on the ball but also for teammates trying to support him.

Breaking the Limits of One-Footedness

I have tried to demonstrate the advantages of two-footedness, or the ability to play the ball to any direction with either foot. Through years of close observation of players at all levels of the game, I am convinced that a player who is truly two-footed has twice the playing options of the out and out one-footer, and is therefore twice as effective, twice as dangerous to the opposition, and indeed, with all other factors being equal, twice the player. Nowadays there is a problem, the good players can be better in so many ways. They stand out more because they tend to keep the ball more than anyone else. But is that good for the team when the game ends 0 – 0 or 1 – 1? That is the obvious question. Let's take a sobering look at what is really going on during the game of soccer. This information may get coaches to think twice before they simply leave things to mother nature. As I have said before, what looks great on the soccer pitch may not be effective from a team perspective. Will the team benefit from the individual who is a star in the popular eye? Such questions must be answered by examining the reality on the pitch.

Touch Options
The Forward Touch

The lack of two - footedness is a serious issue from a development point of view. The forward touch to the ball and moving the ball off the line are great skills to have, but only if the player can comfortably perform them with both feet. The out and out one footed player will always have half the options on the pitch of a player who is two-footed.

Most great players certainly know how to play the forward touch. However, the out and out one footedness of the players will always be a problem from a team point of view. Keeping the ball on the right foot all the time sometimes makes players look good because they have taken ten touches to the ball and made themselves look good in front of the cameras. But what about the team? In fact, getting a lot of practice working on the one good foot is the problem!

Lets Examine - The Comfort Zone

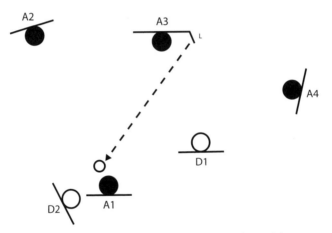

The Effective Truth – Lost Playing Options Diagram

In the above line up, the position of the players can be considered to be a fragment from a playing system, seen from the air. Meaning that the line up should be familiar – A3 is part of the central defensive unit (back four). I could easily name names but that wouldn't be fair. The center back in this example is a famous player. I watched this player for a number of months. I was not surprised to see that players with a one footedness disposition hardly ever played the ball to their weak side, in the case of our friend it was his left side. Strange when you know that this player is left footed. Player A3 would rarely play the ball to his left. The midfield player A4 would hardly get a look from A3. This is why I am looking at what is going on from a playing point of view. There are lots of moments during the game that say everything to me about the lack of two - footedness on the ball in most players. What players did more often than they should is to play what is known as the percentage game – to knock the ball long. The player I observed did a lot of that, which in effect put 'his own' players under pressure. Most players play to their strength. The problem is that their strength is also in effect their greatest weakness.

Further Explanation
Making Decisions

The skill of playing soccer depends on the input of the coaching methods. To keep things "natural" is nothing but a cop out. It is simply wrong. Wrong because some players never reach their true playing potential. Being two footed and knowing how to play the skills to good effect is the business of playing soccer. Players can only play the way they have been taught. Instinctive or otherwise, it is the input over the years that actually results in a good, bad, or indifferent player.

It is very important to know that all development or lack of development leads to the way the player plays the game of soccer. In taking the forward touch to the ball, the player committed himself to the playing options that were in fact effectively almost set in stone. The player didn't realize it but his starting position in his working sequence of taking the forward touch and then moving forward by speeding up the physical movements displayed a lack of development from a playing point of view. His actions thanks to his own one - footedness and therefore years of hard work on that foot had made him like an aeroplane that's taking off. Once forward moving and committed to his action the player cant change his mind. Just like the plane going fast down the runway, the plane has no option but to take off with all its consequences. It happens to be true that the one footedness of the player is forcing his hand and making him play the ball to his comfort zone, which is forward and diagonal from his position.

The least comfortable option in the player's mind would be to play the pass to the angle that would place him sideways on to the natural forward moving game. That thought process would be two footed. The two footed player would be able to think left or right. In examining the Comfort Zone Diagram the better playing options were lost. If the pass was played to player A4 he could have taken on the one defensive player in front of him and made it a 3v1 by joining up with player A1.

In Conclusion – The two footed player has twice the playing options of a one footed player and thus is able to play more effective soccer. Future coaching methods have to empower the player to play the more effective game of

94

soccer. Yes! The two footedness of the player together with his playing skills is a quest worth pursuing. Knowing first touch options and being two footed is the key to the player's future. Systems of play are important but let's get it right. It is the players and their talent that make all the difference and not the system of play on paper.

The Extended Touch

This is an effective touch because it can be played to a 90° angle and if the player is two footed it gives him a 180° angle playing capability. The simplicity of the skill is that it is easy to play and control the ball but very difficult in certain playing circumstances for the opponents to get to the ball. The extended foot inside instep out-turned position to the ball is especially useful when the opponents are marking players tight goal side.

In Practice Mode

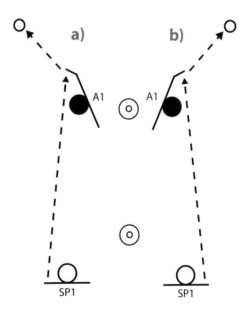

a) A1 receives the pass from SP1 and cushions the ball with the inside instep of his right foot, moving the ball on the first touch to the angle shown.

a) A1 receives the pass from SP1 and cushions the ball with the inside instep of his left foot, moving the ball on the first touch to the angle shown.

In Playing Mode
The Extended Touch

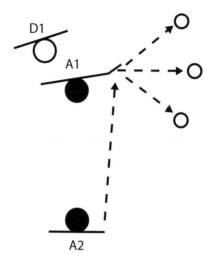

The Extended Foot Position

Player A1 in taking this touch can turn around against the defensive position, almost going around the corner if you like, to the back of D1.
The body follows the foot. The touch using the inside instep can take the ball to several angles without risking possession of the ball to player D1. The angle of the touch depends on the strength of touch and the direction of the toe.

The Practice Format
The Set Up Touch

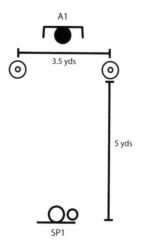

The working format for the practice of setting the ball up for another play option is similar to the off the line touch and the extended touch format.

In Practice Mode

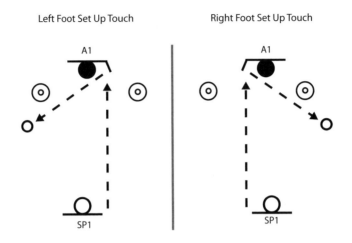

Left Foot Set Up Touch   Right Foot Set Up Touch

A1   A1

SP1   SP1

Practice Objectives - The pass is made to the left or right inside instep of player A1. The inside instep is slightly offset from the natural foot position. The touch on the ball moves the ball to the angle shown.

In Play Mode
The Forward Touch & Set Up Touch Options

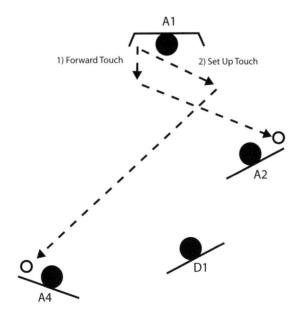

A1

1) Forward Touch   2) Set Up Touch

A2

A4   D1

Player A1 has noticed the run of player A4, but because it requires a long pass, his first touch must be used to 'set up' the ball and his body position to effectively play the long ball.

1 – The forward touch, taken with the inside instep of the right foot, could place the ball to the correct angle for the diagonal pass to player A4. The touch angle of the set up can allow the player to use more strength to the pass. Look at the position of player A4 – If the distance is out of reach for the short pass option then in that case the set up touch comes into effect. Player A1 sets the ball up with the inside instep of the foot to the angle 2 and plays the long ball to player A4 with his right foot (preferably laces to the ball) – The angle of the set up touch places the ball to an angle that is compatible to the laces part of the boot. Striking the ball with the laces part of the boot is always more effective in terms of playing the long ball because the foot position and therefore the leg position to the ball is more swing effective, so to speak.

One More Touch Option
The Reverse Touch Option

This next touch example is called the 'Reverse Touch Option' - Unlike all the first touch options mentioned thus far the foot does not follow through but actually withdraws on contact with the ball. This is also a great time to introduce the four-cone placements format.

Practice Mode
The Reverse Touch

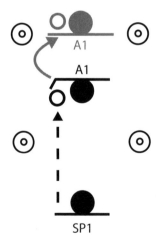

98

RIGHT & LEFT FOOT –

SP1 plays the ball to the player A1 – A1 takes the ball on the inside instep of the right or left foot, cushioning the pass while withdrawing the foot and turns on the touch of the ball.

We have worked on some of the more relevant ball control and ground playing options in the game of soccer. It is possible to play the next man into the center by means of rotation. Set players outside of the format in order to work out a pass and move scenario where the players take turns practicing all the functional elements, such as taking the first touch to the ball.

All Touch Options

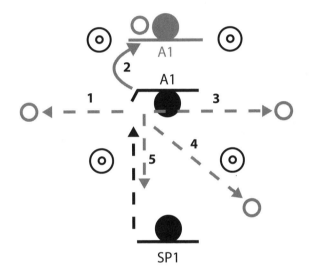

Only right foot touch options shown for clarity

1- Extended Foot Touch
2 - Reverse Touch
3 - Moving the Ball Off the Line
4 - Set Up Touch
5 - Forward Touch

We can take all the touch options into the above format and work the touches as starting points to the practice of passing the ball and therefore the whole range of considerations that we have discussed thus far. If you review the one on one skills to the outside of the four cone placements and add all you know about the first touch options that we have discussed, you will see how easy it is to work on all of that in the above format.

In Terms Of Other Playing Solutions

The touches taken to the ball and the pass of the ball are obviously linked to form effective playing solutions - Playing the ball to feet, playing the ball to space, playing the ball to the right foot, playing the ball to the left foot etc. Such details are important in developing higher standards of play. Does it matter which foot the ball should be played to? Yes it does! It is important to realize that no matter what the system of play it is the ability of the player that wins games. There is a system of play within the system of play, namely the pass. The game of soccer is based on the pass and effective touches on the ball. The two go hand in hand and that's why playing the pass and considering what happens to the pass is important. The two footedness of the player makes the game, it doesn't break the game. If the players have more playing options they can play better, simple as that. The definition of the first touch together with the understanding of the function of the pass will deliver a higher standard of play.

In Playing Mode

D1

A2

"Man on!"

If the ball is played to the receiving player A2 in a way that doesn't favor either foot , it can be the signal to A2 that A1 wants the ball back on first contact.

A1

It is simply correct to suggest that if the players are two footed and therefore capable of playing the ball with either foot, they can then use the skills on offer to their advantage. It is also true to say that the game of soccer is a language of its own and to play the game effectively a player must be able to read this soccer language. Coaches often talk about the players having to talk to each other, but there is a way that players can speak to each other without saying a word. It is called the language of the pass. If the players are two footed it is possible to talk to each other by passing the ball to certain effect. Passing the ball to the left foot or to the right foot or to the neutral unbiased front of the player position and even to the side of the player can speak volumes. Each pass option sends its own message. In the next example the players are talking to each other. It's a question of reading the position of the opponents when in possession of the ball. In this next example Player A2 can see what is behind player A1 so he knows A1 is marked on his right shoulder. The pass can be made to A1 even if he is marked because the pass can be made to his left foot and if the player has a decent first touch (like the extended touch), then there should be no problems.

In Playing Mode
The Biased Pass

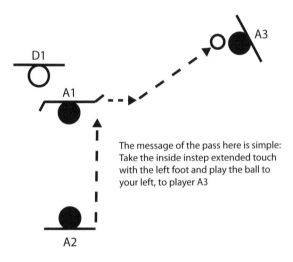

The message of the pass here is simple: Take the inside instep extended touch with the left foot and play the ball to your left, to player A3

One-footed players wouldn't dream of passing the ball to a marked player. My point is that the two footedness of the player makes it possible to think differently. The biased pass to the left foot makes it possible for the player to keep the ball away from player D1 by taking the touch to the square on angle. Playing the ball to a specific target/foot is very important at times. The pass to the correct foot makes all the difference from a playing point of view. Playing the ball to the right or the left foot or simply to feet or even to the side of the player could tell the receiving player which way he should play the ball in order to open up his attacking options. In higher standards of play the biased pass to the left foot or the right foot is made after reading the position of the defensive players. Playing the ball to a specific foot (right or left foot) helps the receiving player set his next playing solution.

Affecting Playing Standards

If the pass is made in such a way that it considers the position of the opponents, the attacking side of the game becomes more effective. Here are a few more examples illustrating the importance of being 'Two footed'.

Fast Turns & Take Ups

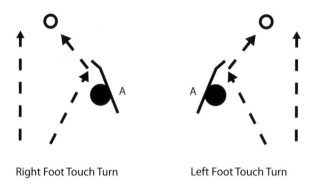

Right Foot Touch Turn   Left Foot Touch Turn

Some of the simplest of turns can not be accomplished if the player is only capable of using one foot to the ball. Of course, even the out and out one footer could eventually turn in any direction, but in one direction he would need multiple touches on the ball to accomplish what the two footed player can do with one or two touches in any direction. Obviously, more touches will take more time and the pace of the move and subsequently the game will suffer. The problem of one footedness is a real issue, affecting even what goes on within the playing system itself.

Chapter 9 - DRIBBLING SKILLS

The two footedness of the player is never more clear than in the following examples of working formats that deal with the development of the player's ability to take a meaningful touch to the ball with either the left or the right foot. Taking a touch and playing off the first touch gives the player the opportunity to develop fast feet and good ball control skills. The following formats consider the use of appropriate working elements that complete the make-up of the training environment for the development of two-footedness.

PRACTICE & PLAYING MODE
PLAYING OFF THE FIRST TOUCH

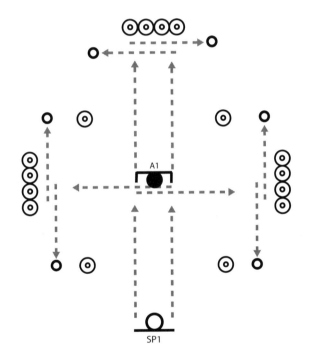

IN PRACTICE & PLAYING MODE

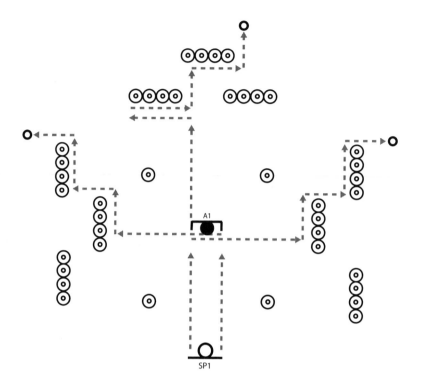

DEVELOP FAST FEET FOR TAKING ON THE SECOND CHALLENGER

FAST FEET COMBINATIONS

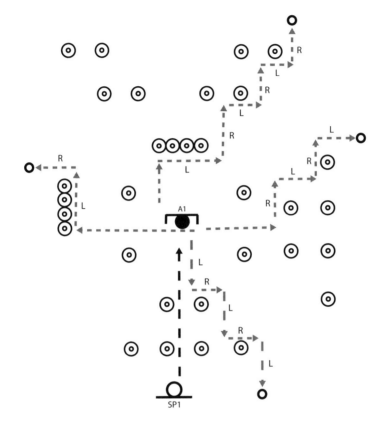

Player A1 takes the first touch to the ball using one of the first touch options: forward touch, off the line touch, extended touch, reverse touch, etc. and takes on the second "defender" using fast feet skills such as the sweep or inverted steps. In effect, we are presenting to the player challenges he will encounter in a real match and equipping him with the tools he will need to meet those challenges, all in a controlled environment where he can perform the skills in a repetitive fashion for maximum effect.

Dribbling Skills – FOR TAKING ON MORE THAN ONE CHALLENGER

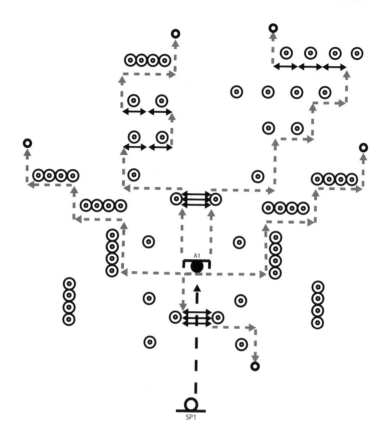

The above format deals with a combination of fast touches and slower touches. Fast touches are with the short inside instep movements and the slower touches to the ball are the inside instep touches that move the ball off the line. SP1 plays the ball in – Player A1 takes the appropriate first touch and affects his one on one play options.

Note - The end game of any training session can be to practice one on one skills by actually working the skills developed in the practice into a game-like format.

Two Footedness Finishing

Finishing Off The First Touch - & Finishing off 'One on One Skills'

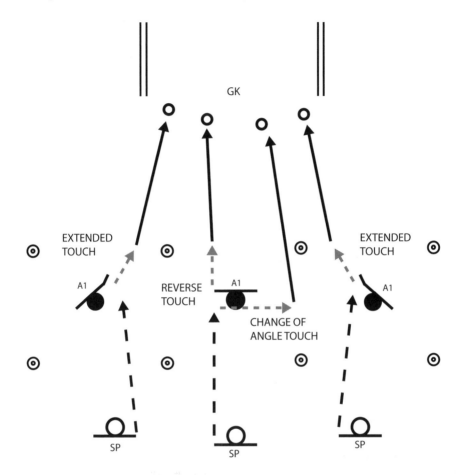

Player A1 - Take the first touch options as your starting point for taking the touch to the ball and striking it with the appropriate foot.

Finishing – One On One

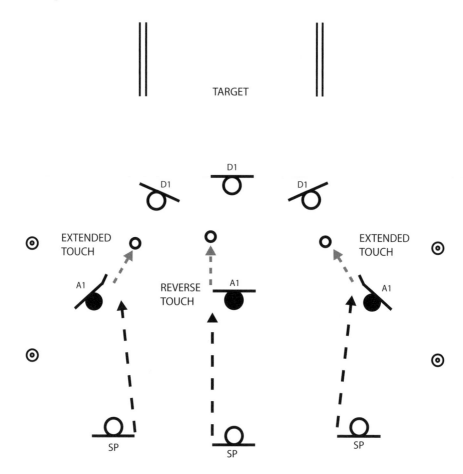

TARGET

What do you see? I see the A1 taking an extended touch which puts him in direct conflict with the defensive player D1.

I can see the left foot reverse touch and the right foot reverse touch and that touch takes the attacking player into a direct line of attack against the defensive player D1. SP1 plays the ball to player A1 – Player A1 works on taking the touch that puts him into conflict situations where he will apply his One On One skills to create goal scoring opportunities. The player will be encouraged to take a touch and speed up to the defensive position. To go past the defensive position, to the side of and finish.

End Of Training

Conclusion

First of all thank you for taking this journey with me and taking a look at the working formats that deal with the development of the two - footedness of the player and the individual skills that help the player play effective soccer.

I have worked on the above issues for many years and have come to the conclusion that in fact there are no excuses for the one footedness of the player, save one. Namely; That the player has never had the opportunity to work on his/her two - footedness. There are, obviously problems of-course. The problem is that none of them can be dealt with on a part time basis. The development of the players two footedness is down to hard work and to working in the appropriate method of training. The first port of call in my work was the development of the strength of the right and left side of the player, physically speaking. It goes without saying that I did that work within the lateral development format that I titled 'The Single Line Of Cones'. Formats of this nature alone can develop the player's psychological and physical acceptance of the use of the so-called weak side of the player. The fight against the habitual effects of the forward moving world is not to be taken lightly. The one footedness of the player does lead to a lesser playing ability. It is therefore my intention in this book to highlight the issues surrounding the lack of two footedness in the playing soccer domain and to give the reader the opportunity to solve the lack of two footedness problem that besets some players today.

My Best Wishes
M Bidzinski